Signs of the Times

Signs of the Times

*The Secret Lives of
Twelve Everyday Icons*

Peter Graystone

CANTERBURY
PRESS
Norwich

© Peter Graystone 2004

First published in 2004 by the Canterbury Press Norwich
(a publishing imprint of Hymns Ancient &
Modern Limited, a registered charity)
St Mary's Works, St Mary's Plain,
Norwich, Norfolk, NR3 3BH

www.scm-canterburypress.co.uk

Unless otherwise indicated, Bible quotations are
taken from the *New International Version* © 1973,
1978, 1984 by the International Bible Society.
Published by Hodder & Stoughton.

British Library Cataloguing in Publication data

A catalogue record for this book is available
from the British Library

ISBN 1-85311-566-5

Typeset by Regent Typesetting, London
Printed and bound by
Bookmarque, Croydon, Surrey

For Paul, obviously

Contents

I

Introduction

'Read the signs of the times!' said Jesus.

The Pharisees had come to him demanding that he should prove his claims by performing a miracle – one of many occasions on which they did so. Repeatedly Jesus refused to co-operate, but on one occasion he explained why it frustrated him so much:

> When evening comes, you say, 'It will be fair weather, for the sky is red,' and in the morning, 'Today it will be stormy, for the sky is red and overcast.' You know how to interpret the appearance of the sky, but you cannot interpret the signs of the times. A wicked and adulterous generation looks for a miraculous sign, but none will be given it except the sign of Jonah.[1]

Jesus seemed to be saying that everything that those who were searching wanted to know about his nature could be worked out from what was clearly visible in the world and in his ministry. It would take more than a miracle to open the eyes of people so blind that they could not see the signs of God at work that were so evident around them. And the example he gave was one that has lost none of its interest as the centuries rolled on – the weather forecast. 'Red sky at night, shepherds' delight; red sky in the morning, shepherds' warning.' I have known about that sign since before I went to school! Our ability to forecast the weather has improved beyond measure over two thousand years; our ability to read the spiritual signs of the times is more patchy.

This book looks at a dozen images that have become iconic at the beginning of the twenty-first century. They are ubiquitous – a tattooed shoulder, a lamp-post covered in dying flowers, a plastic card at a supermarket check-out, the logos that brand merchandise. Where have they come from? Why do we need them? What does it say about the nation that they are so prevalent that we have stopped noticing them? And what can we learn about our spirituality from their popularity?

The book is heading toward two icons which, because of the life and death of Jesus, have become signs for all times. The penultimate chapter is about the cross, which is examined not for its theological meaning but to investigate whether it still has power as an image when it is on display alongside the swoosh, the golden arches, and all the other logos that speak to us without words. The final chapter is about the empty tomb (or as Jesus called it 'the sign of Jonah' – the man who, in the Bible story, emerged blinking into the light after three deathly days inside a huge fish). How and where do they appear as visual images in our society? Have they held or lost their iconic power? How can Christian people find in them the inspiration to live with faith in a post-Christian society? And how did the cross of Jesus' execution come to be the logo so recognizable that advertisers would kill for its brand recognition, rather than the empty tomb which speaks of the resurrection that is central to faith?

I do hope that reading the signs of the times will inspire you to look at the world around you in a slightly different way. And I hope that at the end of it you will come to the same conclusion as me – that those who engage with the culture in the way Jesus encouraged us to will end up rejoicing because they find it buzzing with the rumours of God.

Note

1 Matthew 16:1–3.

2

The Tattoo

The answer to your first question is: 'No I haven't.'

I don't think I would either, not even if I was twenty years younger and it was the ultimate fashion statement of the moment. Which, of course, it is! It is the commitment I couldn't cope with. Now that is *very* twenty-first century!

Commitment comes no more easily to me than to anyone else whose values are shaped by the age in which we live. If I am in a job for more than three years I convince myself that I have gone stale. I am frequently bored with all my clothes, all my music, and I can't find a single book on my overflowing shelves that I want to read. I have even found myself complaining to God that there are not enough colours in the spectrum because I have seen the ones I like already. It is a miracle, which I put down to grace alone, that I have kept a relationship with God alive for two decades, so you can imagine how unlikely it is that I will decorate myself with something that is absolutely never going to go.

But Bjork has got one. It is on her arm and it is a Norse symbol like a snowflake. It signifies seeking strength for the future in the cultural hinterland of your ancestry. Drawing on Iceland's rich mythological heritage, it seems appropriate to her. However, my cultural heritage is Croydon, and it is difficult to know what kind of strength one is supposed to draw from that!

Robbie Williams has many. His arm looks like a cheese grater. He has got two with words in them. One reads 'Elvis grant me serenity' and the other reads 'Born to be mild'. It is interesting that in both cases he has chosen words that allude to Christian sayings. I wonder what he yearns after.

David Beckham has five. At least, he has five that you could see in that infamous publicity shoot, and it is difficult to imagine where he would put one that isn't already on show. He has got his son's name, Brooklyn, at the base of his spine. He has got his wife Victoria's name on his forearm, written in Hindi (although apparently there is an embarrassing mistake in one of the characters). I won't tell you what is on his chest because I think there are some things that ought to remain private between a man and his one million readers of the *News of the World*.

Mika Salo, lead driver for the Toyota Formula One team, has one on his finger. It looks like a twig about to burst into leaf, and it encircles the fourth finger of his left hand in the place where one might expect to see a wedding ring. His wife Noriko has one too, in exactly the same position. They were tattooed together on the day of their marriage.

Tom Cruise has reputedly paid a fortune for laser treatment to have NK removed from one buttock, but the gossip columns have not revealed whether PC has appeared on the other.

Geri Halliwell's tattoo disappeared overnight, which seems slightly unfair on the legions of teenage girls who managed to scrape together enough money from their Saturday jobs to copy her first decision, but will never earn enough to copy her second decision. This leads to the strange prospect, sixty years hence, of a generation of elderly ladies in nursing homes with grey and wrinkled smudges that they assure the nurses used to be roses and birds.

Lloyd Cole sings of the ultimate embarrassment – the girl who promised that the relationship would last forever, but moved on and became just an indelible 'Jennifer' written in blue underneath a heart and an arrow on his arm.[1]

Could anyone have predicted ten years ago that the tattoo would become the major fashion statement of the beginning of the twenty-first century?

Obviously tattooing has an honourable tradition. Every culture in the history of the world has at some point found it attractive to decorate the body by marking it or piercing it or stretching it in some way. And I have no doubt that our Celtic ancestors hunting on the mountains in wode would recognize in the tattoos of today the spirit of what was found beautiful centuries ago. We now deplore Victorian missionaries who went to Africa and were so shocked by what they saw that they insisted new converts to Christianity combed their hair and hid their body-painting under skirts. Through the goodness of God some lessons have been learnt from history. Perhaps that is why there are no Christians picketing tattoo parlours denouncing what is going on inside as the work of Satan.

However, tattooing also has a dishonourable history. It has been used to brand slaves and to number prisoners or workers in concentration camps. It has become useful to people who perpetrate evil as a way of dehumanizing others, permanently diminishing their dignity until they cease to be personalities and become someone else's numbered property. It may be in this context, or simply to make the worship of the Hebrews distinct from heathen practices, that the Old Testament Law forbade the practice: 'Do not cut your bodies for the dead or put tattoo marks on yourselves. I am the Lord.'[2]

The kind of tattooing we know today has its roots in eighteenth-century Polynesian society, and Europeans first encountered it when the accounts and pictures of James Cook's voyage to Tahiti came to Britain. Joseph Banks, the naturalist who accompanied Cook on his first voyage to the Pacific Ocean recorded this:

> I shall now mention their methods of painting their bodies, or tattow as it is called in their language. They do this by inlaying black under their skin in such a manner as to be indelible. Everyone is thus marked in different parts of his body according to his humour or different circumstances of his life . . . I saw this operation performed on the buttocks of a girl about fourteen years of age. For some time she bore it with great resolution, but afterwards began to complain, and in little time grew so outrageous that all the threats and force her friends could use hardly obliged her to endure it.[3]

In the islands of the South Pacific, tattooing was not mere decoration, but had a deeply spiritual significance. The tiny, detailed flecks and curls of patterning that made up Samoan tattoos were held to protect the bearer from the dangers of the spiritual world by sealing all that was sacred within the body. In Tahiti, broad areas of black imposed on the buttocks and around the genitals were a rite of passage, indicating that boys and girls had reached puberty and could enter certain social and sexual relationships without risking spiritual injury to themselves or others. It seems that the pain involved in achieving the tattoo was as vital a part of the experience as the finished result. The bravado required is doubtless still part of people's motivation today, although it is worth remembering that in Polynesia the tattoo was created with a chisel, hammer and crude ink with only the encouragement of watching friends as an anaesthetic!

Christian missionaries arrived first in the Polynesian islands in 1797, and by 1850 the islanders were largely converted to Christianity. The London Missionary Society, as you would anticipate, saw tattoos as indicative of a sinful life and urged converts to repent of them. Because of their permanence, the islanders bore the guilt they felt for what they'd done innocently in early life in a very obvious way. However, children brought up in the Christian faith were kept free from tattoos. Those who broke the prohibition were punished by being scoured with sandstone until their skin was torn away. The missionaries encouraged the association between tattooing and sin by changing its use. They used the techniques to brand criminals as a punishment, for instance imposing the word 'thief' on an offender's face. There is a line of shame that stretches indelibly from concentration camp commandants to Christian missionaries.

However, as fast as European Christianity was putting converts into trousers, a cultural exchange was happening of its own accord. It took less than thirty years for a tattoo to become essential fashion for sailors world-wide. A new kind of imagery developed, making less use of abstract designs and more of recognizable shapes and pictures – often maritime images. At the trial following the mutiny on board the *Bounty*, Captain Bligh used tattoos which had been gained in Tahiti to identify the mutineers. For the record, Fletcher Christian had a cross on his chest and an anchor on his buttock.

In the nineteenth and early twentieth centuries it became a widespread practice for sailors to have an image of the crucifixion of Jesus tattooed across their backs. The thinking behind this was that a sea captain, no matter how harsh, would not dare order the lash to be administered to the image of Christ. The spiritual protection which the indigenous Polynesian religions had offered through tattoos had been absorbed in a much more practical way by the Christian religion – not as taught, but as lived. (Tattooed images of Jesus have endured in popularity. Phil Taylor, who has been darts world-champion ten times, sports the crucified Jesus on his right calf. Curiously, the footballer Diego Maradona has Fidel Castro in exactly the same place.)

In 1882 the future King George V created a remarkable precedent by having the image of a dragon tattooed while he was in the Far East. (He was seventeen. Under present-day legislation he would have to wait another year to be tattooed in the UK.) For a brief period, high-quality tattoos became fashionable among the upper classes as a result of this. However, this was much against the tide of belief about the appropriateness of the practice. In fact, criminologists such as Cesare Lombroso interpreted the desire to brand oneself in this way as evidence of 'a degenerate and primitive mentality that arose from the bad breeding of the socially and biologically inferior classes',[4] and the presence of a tattoo was sometimes offered in court as evidence of criminally inclined character.

For fifty years after the turn of the century tattooing was almost exclusively associated with the navy or the military – a badge of pride in your ship or patriotic fervour, or a tribute to your lover back home. It was something accepted and perhaps respected (an unspoken acknowledgement of having served one's country during war). However, it was definitely a male adornment, and almost exclusively working class again. In fact John F. Kennedy had one that he picked up as a young subaltern of which he was ashamed later in life because he felt it was beneath the dignity of someone who had risen to become President of the United States.

It was during the second half of the twentieth century that groups on the fringes of society adopted tattooing as a mark of clan identity. Anyone who was in his or her heyday in the 1960s or 1970s associated tattoos almost exclusively with Hell's Angels, or later with skinheads. It was part of a revival in the art which emanated from California (again, starting in the seaports). By the 1980s it was almost entirely associated with the tribal instincts of urban youth, and with being aggressively at odds with society.

So it would have been difficult to anticipate that this was going to develop, in the last few years, into a fashion worn with dignity across a large demographic range – a mainstream style accessory sported by a broad spectrum of the population. And it would have been well-nigh impossible to foresee that its main appeal would be to the middle classes, and that women would be inclined to decorate themselves with a tattoo as much as (and amongst hardcore nightclubbers, more than) men. But that is the case, and any lingering doubts about it were swept aside in June 2003 when Selfridges department store in London, that shrine to respectable middle-class aspiration, opened its own booth – Zulu Tattoo.

Jon Simmons runs a tattoo parlour in Central London. Not only does he see himself as an artist, he has a degree to prove it. There is not a centimetre of pink left on him! His suite is not dingy or threatening, as one might have expected ten years ago. It is bright and clean, with magazines to read in the waiting room and high-class advertising on the walls. In fact, it looks like a dentist's waiting room. It is a place designed to make a middle-class consumer feel at home. I say hallo to him every time I walk past, because he stands outside to smoke a cigarette. Obviously, for hygiene reasons he is not allowed to smoke inside his studio. However, environmental health regulations will not allow smoking in the waiting room either, because his assistant serves cappuccino there.

In 1992 he visited New Zealand to research traditional Maori designs and techniques of body decoration, which were undergoing a revival. In remote places such as Samoa the practice had never been completely suppressed, despite the best efforts of the missionaries. Jon Simmons speaks zealously of the function of the tattoo (and specifically of designs with spiritual significance in the traditions of indigenous peoples) as running counter to the materialist culture of developed nations. The tone of his voice is almost religious as he describes the experience of getting and giving a tattoo as transcendent. It has, he says, grounded his sense of 'home' in his own body. He sees it as a way of surrendering one's body to a mark of something higher and of more value than consumerism. 'A mobile phone is for show, but a tattoo is for life.'

Jon sees the renaissance of the tattoo as one part of a 'modern primitivism' which, feeling let down by organized religion, seeks inspiration in aboriginal religions and paganism. However, he scorns those who seek motifs that have significance in the heritage of ancient peoples solely because of their aesthetic value. (In this respect Celtic, Maori and Chinese designs are of the moment.) He is proud, he says, to mark people with images that they have chosen 'not because they are pretty, but to create a beautiful cultural exchange'. And his cheeks glow blue with admiration when he reflects on the decoration of Robbie Williams' shoulder, which was described earlier: 'Not static, but a living thing – curling and spiralling.' It is, he reveals, the work of the Polynesian artist Te Rangitu Netana, regarded as the greatest living exponent of his craft. (I should not have described it so dismissively in the opening paragraphs!) Looking to the future, Jon points out that being incorporated into a fashion system that expresses identity and spirituality, the present role of the tattoo might be understood sympathetically by men and women who lived in the South Pacific islands two hundred years ago.

Nicholas Thomas, however, doubts that the tattoo will ever be accepted as a 'safe' fashion accessory. In his book *Skin Deep* he points out that, historically, a period of acceptance of tattoos has always prompted new ways of shocking people with the imagery:

> Urban youth is creating new tattoo styles that draw their imagery . . . from graffiti. These kinds of development indicate that tattooing has not simply become incorporated into some fashionable system that threatens or offends no one.[5]

In what way is it a sign of the times that the concept of tattooing, which may be as old as time itself, is suddenly the nation's hottest fashion? Thinking about that question has drawn me back to the Bible. Tattooing is a biblical metaphor. Its most memorable use is by Paul, who employed it to describe a characteristic of the Holy Spirit:

> You were included in Christ when you heard the word of truth, the gospel of your salvation. Having believed, you were marked in him with a seal, the promised Holy Spirit, who is a deposit guaranteeing our inheritance until the redemption of those who are God's possession – to the praise of his glory.[6]

'Marked with a seal' is the Hebrew word for tattooed or branded. Christians have been tattooed with the Holy Spirit, an invisible but absolutely permanent mark of belonging to God. Shoppers in the market place thirty years after Jesus did not purchase their goods from Tesco in pre-packed containers containing just enough for two; they bought goods in substantial quantities! Sackfuls of produce, livestock still live and refusing to be stock still, and perhaps even humans! Goods bought at the beginning of a day would be tattooed with a personal brand. Being indelibly and permanently marked with a sign showed that they belonged to one owner and were unavailable to anyone else until they were collected by the customer at the end of the day. The tattoo was a deposit that guaranteed ownership.

Committed ownership is the concept about which Paul is talking. As Christians purchased by God at enormous expense – it cost the life of his Son – we can never, absolutely never, be taken from him to belong to anyone else. How can anyone tell? Because we have been tattooed with the Holy Spirit – invisible, but straightforwardly obvious to God, and increasingly obvious to anyone who sees that the influence of God's ownership of our lives changes us for the better. It is God's deposit on us guaranteeing that, on the day we meet him, he will be able to say without fear of contradiction: 'That man, that woman, that child is mine – and there is the sign which proves it.'

For the Christian that is an exhilarating truth. Somewhere hidden about your person is a mark invisible to everyone but God – a unique and extraordinary tattoo which is your guarantee that you will join him in Heaven. You can't roll up your sleeve and point it out to people. You have to find other ways of showing them. Old fashioned ways like 'love, joy, peace, patience, kindness, goodness, faithfulness, gentleness and self-control'.[7] Against such things there is no law, and against such things there is no stereotypically British reserve. And there never will be!

There never will be, because a tattoo is totally permanent. It is never going to change without extreme and expensive difficulty. So, as a sign of the times, it can speak to us of God's irrevocable commitment to us. To ordinary and undeserving members of a changeable and fashion-conscious society! That commitment is never going to weaken until we are his own close possession, as Paul remarkably puts it: 'to the praise of his glory'.

However, the biggest surprise about the rise and rise of the tattoo in the last few years is that it has happened at a time when we are led to believe that commitment of any kind is a diminished concept. Young people, so it is said, are not prepared to commit themselves to marriage. They are not prepared to commit themselves to relationships over a long term. The concept of a job for life is yesterday's. The concept of living in one town for life is that of a previous generation. We have disposable everything. We recycle into something new and different. We make dates and then text people to change the arrangements at the last minute because we get a better offer.

Commitment, so we are told, simply does not figure in the make-up of our society. Except for tattoos! A person who is in every way a child of this generation will freely make a decision to commit himself or herself for all time to a fashion statement.

As a Christian that thrills me! Sometimes I feel that we are on the verge of giving up expecting people to commit themselves in faith for a lifetime because it runs against the spirit of the age. But the tattoo tells us not to give up hope in the gospel message which we hold out – that the way God intended us to live is in permanent, life-enhancing commitment to him. There are still some things that people deem so valuable that they are prepared to invest their whole lives in them. A new tattoo is one. The gospel of new life, new hope, new expectations, new joy can be another.

What is it that can draw out of people this heroic, all-embracing commitment to God? It is his gratuitous, all-forgiving commitment to us. And if we ever have cause to doubt it the Holy Spirit, his deposit within us, is the guarantee that he is our owner.

Alison Lyon has a tattoo. I haven't seen it, but several years of working as colleagues have made me sure that I can take her at her word. And besides, I joined thousands of others to hear the whizz of the drill on Radio 4's *Home Truths*. She wanted to mark the twentieth anniversary of her recovery from cancer. Among the few physical signs left of her fight against the illness were the irremovable blue marks that had been put on her torso, front and back, to line up the machines that delivered therapeutic radiography. They themselves were tattoos, and they were a memory of a bad thing. So she decided to have the marks incorporated into a design of her own choosing that would be full of symbolism as a sign of thanksgiving.

Ali told me, 'The little dots that remain from my treatment are not that unsightly, but they are quite obvious and they are not self-explanatory. One reason for the tattoo was to draw attention away from them on to something that doesn't require a medical life history to explain. It is a green spiral which, for me, is a very godly symbol. Both the shape (in and out, out and in, on and on) and the colour (fertility, which technically I do not have because my ovaries were wrecked by the treatment) are important to me.'

Her friends have found it inspiring that she has chosen to redeem something scarring and indelible into something beautiful and full of meaning. It is a reflection of the God in whom we believe – faithful through bad times and good, and always at work on a project to bring good out of evil on earth. And he is ultimately intent on 'bringing all things in heaven and on earth together under one head, namely Christ', as Paul puts it when he writes about being tattooed by the Holy Spirit.[8]

Throughout history, the way the body has been presented has never been wholly natural. It has always been modified and groomed for social reasons. And in equal measure, the way it has been manipulated has been either to express social norms or to exclude a person from them. But tattooing is unique in this because of its enduring quality – not just adorning people but creating illustrated men and women.

There is, however, one word of caution to add before we rejoice in the possibility of commitment in the twenty-first century. Just recently something insidious has sneaked its way into fashion. It is called the temporary tattoo. It looks like the real thing, but after six weeks it fades away to leave not a mark behind. It is made with henna, or from some kind of chemical transfer, and it is only applied to the surface instead of being drilled indelibly into the skin. People who want the style but not the commitment can have a tattoo safely in the knowledge that if they change their mind, they can change their appearance too. In fact, looking at some of the rock stars who are so conscious of moving with the fashion of the moment, one cannot help but wonder whether some of them have cheated! Is it possible that when we see the shoulders of some celebrities after the craze has moved on their tattoos will mysteriously have faded away? Who can tell? Let's wait and see!

There is an insidious brand of spirituality around as well. It is one which says that I can choose what works for me today – a bit of Eastern mysticism, a bit of Buddhism, a bit of Celtic Christianity – knowing that when it stops working I can scrub it away and move on. That is not the gospel of 'hope in Christ for his praise and glory'; that is the gospel of hope for the best because you never know what might happen. It is in startling contrast to what God has done for us. But astonishingly the facts remain the same – even when a person's commitment to God turns out to be a six-week wonder, God's commitment to him or her goes on and on. He is a God of permanence – the Bible calls him 'the Rock', the great unchangeable 'I am'. 'Although we may be faith-less, he remains faithful.'[9]

God, the unchangeable one. Jesus, the one whose commitment to us went as far as death itself. The Holy Spirit, who is the tattoo that has marked us out as God's until the day we meet him face to face. A sign of the times? A sign for all times! Don't be scared to expect commitment in a generation which is obsessed with style, because God was committed first!

Notes

1 'Jennifer She Said', Lloyd Cole and the Commotions, SBK Songs Ltd., 1987.
2 Leviticus 19:28.
3 Joseph Banks, recorded in *The Journals of Captain James Cook*, 1769.
4 Cesare Lombroso, *Crime, its Causes and Remedies*, 1899.
5 Nicholas Thomas, *Skin Deep: A History of Tattooing*, National Maritime Museum, 2002.
6 Ephesians 1:13.
7 Galatians 5:22, 23.
8 Ephesians 1:10.
9 2 Timothy 2:13.

The Loyalty Card

Last week I was taken by surprise to see at the top of my supermarket receipt, 'Thank you, Mr Graystone, for choosing to shop at Tesco today.' My first reaction was: 'Good grief! They know my name!'

My second was: 'Of course! They know it from the store loyalty card which sends me discount vouchers.'

My third was: 'Oh dear! That means they also have a record of whether my purchases included health food and the *Church Times*, or a bottle of gin and *Playboy*.'

My fourth was, 'Who precisely is "they"?'

Nearly three-quarters of consumers in the UK hold a loyalty card of some kind. And among them are a staggering eight million Tesco Clubcard holders, of whom about 80 per cent use it regularly. Every pound spent in a Tesco store generates one reward point. At the check-out, the card is swiped to identify who has spent the money and 'earned' the points. The number of points a customer has accumulated is stored on a computer database. Then, every quarter, he or she is mailed with money-off vouchers equal to £1 for every one hundred points collected. The objective about which the supermarket often tells us is to give us an incentive to shop there regularly. The objective about which they say less is to gather information about us – if you have a loyalty card the company knows your name, address, age, how much you spend, and what you like to buy regularly. And because it knows that, it knows how to tempt you to spend more!

Many stores now offer loyalty cards, but Tesco was the first. Theirs was not, of course, the first scheme to offer rewards to shoppers in order to win their custom away from other stores. The first was actually a store called Pioneers in Rochdale in 1844! In the 1970s a system of bonuses called Green Shield Stamps encouraged allegiance to particular outlets. First at petrol stations, and then at grocery and other stores, customers were offered stamps to paste into collecting books – the more you spent the more you licked. The scheme started life in the United States, but was spectacularly successful in the UK. In every major town was a shop in which books full of stamps could be exchanged for household items – kitchenware, toys, electrical goods and other little luxuries.

At its height it was estimated that two out of every three British women collected Green Shield Stamps. Stores attempted to outbid each other by offering double, triple, even quintuple stamps to customers who favoured them. The quantities involved grew so unwieldy that a larger stamp worth ten smaller ones had to be introduced. A woman whose family saved enough stamps to exchange for a Mini had to hire a lorry to transport the books she had accumulated, and the photo of her delightedly driving the car away became a front page headline on a quiet day for news! A pink rival never achieved the same Green Shield appeal.

But that was all before the days of bar codes, computerized check-outs and tailored marketing. Having turned its back on Green Shield Stamps because they looked tatty and cheap in an age that requires high standards of presentation, Tesco launched the Clubcard in February 1995. They were quickly followed by Safeway. Their accounts show that the card gave them both a substantial competitive advantage in the early months, and Sainsbury's admits that this motivated them to follow with their Reward card. Long before it became the object of a fiercely fought take-over bid Safeway discontinued its scheme, in May 2000, prompting articles in the business pages of newspapers predicting that the phenomenon would not last into the twenty-first century.

But instead they multiply with variations. Sainsbury's joined forces with Debenhams and BP in September 2002 to launch Nectar, which offers a choice between coupons that deduct money from the check-out bill and cumulative points that can be redeemed against gifts and days out for the family. Further brands, including BP and Vodaphone, joined the scheme during 2003. They claim that the co-operation between such high-profile businesses has created the largest affinity card scheme, although this is disputed by Boots who make the claim for their Advantage card (the distinction being whether it is the number of cards in circulation or the number that are actively used which is counted). The long-standing dividend for Co-op purchases can be used either for a reduction in the bill or to donate money to particular charities. For those who fly frequently, Air Miles reward loyal customers, and when the Molton Brown salon chain in West London briefly decided to offer a free haircut after every eight, so did Hair Miles!

But the Tesco Clubcard can certainly make a claim to be the most enduring card of its type. Its magazine of the same name has the highest circulation of any magazine in Europe. The customer relations agency Forward, which devised it, divided the supermarket's adult shoppers into five life stages, each of which gets a different version of the magazine with advertising and features likely to appeal to that consumer group. The information you gave when you innocently filled in your application form for the card dictates which version you receive. And the list of goods you have bought, meticulously catalogued on your receipt, dictates what special offers you are enticed to purchase when your vouchers arrive. You will be offered something that you are naturally inclined to buy, but encouraged to spend slightly more on it than you normally would. The consumer benefits; the store benefits. What a wonderful thing loyalty is!

However, loyalty cards have their detractors. A large number of internet sites are eager to draw our attention to conspiracy theories about what is happening to the information about us to which the card gives access. (I gave up surfing the net as I neared one hundred sites.) Who holds the information? With whom is it shared? How will it be used?

Michael Moore, the maverick film-maker from the USA who is forever nipping at the heels of the political and commercial establishment of the world's only remaining superpower, took to the stage in a live version of his best-selling book *Stupid White Men*. The climax of the show involved the massed on-stage destruction of the loyalty cards of his audience. In a moment of rousing and comical anti-corporate bonding, people enthusiastically surrendered their cards to be shredded in response to Moore's rollicking exhortation for individuals to take back control of their lives in the face of attempts on a massive and enticing scale to surrender information to soulless corporations. It is information, he claims, that might in the long term cost us far more than the value of our discount vouchers.

More scientific approaches also question their true value. The Competition Commission surveyed customers to find out how highly they valued a loyalty card when it came to choosing which supermarket to use. Being able to shop for everything under one roof registered 43 per cent on their scale. Price was the second most important factor at 18 per cent. Among those with lower percentages were range of stock (6 per cent) and flexibility of opening hours (4 per cent). Compared with those, the loyalty card was only mentioned by 5 per cent as a facility which was important to them. Even the state of the toilets registered 18 per cent!

Research into what makes customers return again and again was undertaken in 2000 by the retail consultancy Verdict. They arranged those to whom they talked on a scale of loyalty to particular brands and stores, ranging them from 'advocates' who can't resist telling you how wonderful a product is even if they have to shout it above the music in a nightclub while you are trying to dance, to 'terrorists' who do the reverse when what you would prefer them to do is to get on with driving your taxi or fixing your plumbing.

Having established a scoring system for faithfulness to supermarkets, they found that the two which came out top were Asda (who introduced but then abandoned a card) and Morrisons (who have never had a card, believing that lowering prices is a better incentive). Dr Jonathan Reynolds of the Institute of Retail Marketing at Oxford University, in his lecture 'If you want loyalty get a dog', uses this as evidence that cards are not as effective in marketing as they seem.[1] He holds up 'emotional loyalty' as the nirvana for which companies are searching. It doesn't need a plastic card, or sticky stamps, or any kind of expensive mechanism – it requires a store or brand to win people's hearts. He speaks of 'the chicken factor', picturing what happens when a customer goes into a supermarket shortly before closing time and discovers that there are no chickens in the chiller cabinet. There is what he describes as the American response, which involves the customer haranguing the store manager: 'Hey you! Go this instant to a rival store and buy me a chicken. Then have it sent in a taxi to my front door because it is Thanksgiving and it is outrageous that you have allowed yourself to sell out on a day like today.' The manager goes! That is emotional loyalty to the customer. But there is also the British response, which involves the customer beating himself over the head with a shopping basket and lamenting, 'it is all my fault. Knowing that it was Christmas I should have come an hour earlier to ensure that I got here before the chickens ran out. Now I'll have to buy an inferior one from a shop which is one of your rivals. Can you ever forgive me?' The customer wails! That is emotional loyalty to the store.

Whether or not Jonathan Reynolds is right about the national characteristics, it is interesting that he talks about loyalty in almost religious terms. Perhaps instead of talking about the US and the UK approaches he should talk about the 'righteous anger' and the 'sincere confession' approaches. In the new great religion which is consumerism, loyalty to a particular brand can offer the same sense of security as membership of a church does for Christians. The logo which is printed on a carrier bag or an article of clothing, proudly on show, makes a statement about the kind of person the shopper is and the group he or she belongs to.

The irony is that as fast as having an exclusive allegiance to one particular brand becomes more desirable, having an exclusive allegiance to one particular religion becomes more objectionable. Being openly religious (or at least, openly spiritual) is far more acceptable today than it was in the age of Green Shield Stamps. That was a decade in which talking about your faith at a party was likely to leave you alone in the kitchen sorting out the empty bottles. Now it is likely to push you to the centre of a buzz of conversation with interested, curious, even wistful people. So long as no one tries to interfere in the beliefs (or lack of beliefs) of someone else, it is fine for all the spiritual labels to be on show! Religion has become like underwear. Twenty years ago it was close, personal, and you never talked about it. Nowadays men deliberately wear their trousers loose enough for the brand name to be on show. The only forbidden action is to persuade someone that your Calvin Kleins are acceptable but his Jockeys are pants. In the new religion of consumerism loyalty to a label defines your denomination.

And also your worth! Young people who spend a large proportion of their pocket money and earnings on clothing are doing so for deeper reasons than the need to keep warm. Older people have the same motives, but perhaps pursue them in a more subtle way. In our insistence on choosing the styles or the brands that are appreciated by the group to which we belong, or aspire to belong, we are looking for approval, acceptance, respect. We may be clothing our outsides, but in the choices we make about how to do it, we are addressing our inner lives. Some of us choose clothes so that we will be noticed. Some of us choose them so that we will blend in with others. We want our choices to be remarked on because that increases our esteem. We want to know that we are wearing the right clothes or carrying the most respected accessories for any particular situation because it increases our confidence. Most of us don't want to look as if we are out of place, out of date, or out of cash! These are qualities we need in order to be fulfilled.

Can you buy spiritual values such as esteem, confidence, fulfilment? Well, maybe you can and maybe you can't! Christians come to church looking for precisely those things. The Bible promises us that 'God did not give us a spirit of timidity, but a spirit of power, of love and of self-control.'[2] And these are the very qualities that people are wanting to display when they buy into the promises made by fcuk. Or Nokia. Or Sony. We may insist that seeking worth in a church is superior or longer lasting or more meaningful than seeking it in a shopping mall but, whether we like it or not, it is their spirituality that drives people to both. The cosmetics company L'Oréal sees no point in disguising this and tells me that I should treat myself to products that make me look more desirable, stay eternally young, or just feel better '. . . because I'm worth it!'

Indeed we are worth it! But to put our worth into a proper context we need to gather in a place that reminds us that there is something greater than us which demands our worship. We need a temple!

The Trafford Centre in Manchester is a temple. It is also a cathedral, a pagoda, and (in case living religions alone are not enough to guarantee access to everyone) a pyramid. It has vast, airy spaces to inspire awe. It has domes and pillars and monuments. It even has stained glass. It has beautiful seats to which all those who are weary and heavy laden can come and find rest. It has paths which lead people beside still waters, and I have no doubt that it is holy water which cascades into the pools below. Escalators glide upward for those whose minds are set on higher things. And through its unique programme of 'sensory solutions' the deaf can hear and the blind can see. Under one roof the pilgrim can find leisure, pleasure and the worth that marks his measure. 'Welcome to a stunning world,' the advertising boasts. 'There's never been anything like it.'

I bought socks.

Jill Edwards thinks it is no coincidence that it is possible to describe this profound change in the way we shop by using Christian vocabulary: 'I would like to suggest that we are witnessing, and perhaps participating in an alternative religion.' Jill is chaplain to the Thurrock Shopping Centre in Essex. She has a pastoral role among those who work in the shops, restaurants and entertainment facilities. And for shoppers she makes herself available in the 'quiet place' that has been set aside for reflection or prayer. She has thought and written about the evidence that for some people being a consumer has replaced traditional religion as their main source of solace and comfort:

> Almost everyone understands what is meant by the term 'retail therapy'. People recommend shopping to cheer up the sad, to offer solace to the melancholy, provide company to the lonely, and give a purpose to those whose days are empty. The shopping experience competes with the church as the destination of choice to find the answers to life's problems.[3]

And who is winning? 'Thurrock Shopping centre is open for six hours on a Sunday and about seventy thousand "worshippers" pass through. There isn't a cathedral or church for miles that can even boast a congregation of seven hundred. This presents the Christian Church with an enormous challenge.' She is realistic about how difficult it is for each of us as Christians to turn our back on the prevailing culture of measuring value by what a person owns because it is so satisfying to be sucked into it ourselves. And she points out that powerful people preach in a way that confuses the issues. After the terrorist attack that devastated the heart of New York on 11 September 2001 the Prime Minister of the UK, Tony Blair, urged people not to stay fearfully in their homes, but to go out and shop defiantly in order to demonstrate that no threat of evil could shake our confidence. His words fell on eager ears and pre-Christmas spending on goods exceeded all records in many places. It led the political commentator Sir Bernard Ingham to describe retailers as 'the saviours of the nation'. Jill Edwards adds, tongue evidently in cheek, 'It seems that no problem is too big for the new religion to handle.'

When it comes to suggesting what a Christian response to this might be, she is more inclined to ask questions than to make assertions. She asks us to think about why churches have been unable to present the gospel of Jesus Christ in a way that is convincing to those who are seeking their true identity and want to see themselves as valued. An outward makeover of clothing and lifestyle can make a person feel born again, so how can we witness to ways in which people can find their inner worth in a relationship with Jesus? Convinced that consumerist values are actually fantasies and will be unable to deliver fulfilment in the long term, Jill sees hope in those corners of the Kingdom of God in which the qualities of people who are poor are given honour equal to or greater than those of people who are rich. In such places loyalty is rewarded by more than discounts; it generates the kinds of genuine happiness that are not for sale.

'Loyalty' is not itself a New Testament word. And in the Old Testament it is not really associated with happiness – its presence among soldiers in battle leads to victory; suspicion of its absence leaves kings with sleepless nights. In one of the Psalms, Asaph sings of the difference between the appearance of religious fulfilment and its actual impact in ways that find an echo in Jill Edward's analysis:

> God was their Rock,
> God Most High was their Redeemer.
> But then they would flatter him with their mouths,
> lying to him with their tongues;
> their hearts were not loyal to him,
> they were not faithful to his covenant.[4]

And it is in that psalm that we can find hope that all is not lost for a generation which seeks a new religion to fill the God-shaped void because God, gracious to the last, has never responded to a lack of loyalty in kind:

> Yet he was merciful;
> he forgave their iniquities and did not destroy them.
> Time after time he restrained his anger
> and did not stir up his full wrath.
> He remembered that they were but flesh,
> a passing breeze that does not return.[5]

And yet it has to be admitted that sometimes we have to take the loyalty of God to his people on trust. Those who seek fulfilment for their soul in God sometimes look at those who seek it in material possessions and envy their spontaneity and certainty. Again and again when the really important prayers are being said, our access to God appears to be closed. But we go to bed reassured that Tesco is open twenty-four hours in every day should an emergency arise. The fact of the matter is that God lets us down. A pair of shoes doesn't. Or at least, if there is a problem with the sole they can be changed with no questions asked.

But the religion that looks to Jesus to transform us is different from the religion that looks to the till. It has a different God altogether. It is different because it has a God who has faced up to death. The racks of cosmetics sold by young people in clinical white coats cry out to us with their offer to keep age at bay for those desperate enough to pay. But the Christian God has experienced death, taken its full ferocity, and transformed it. All that money can buy cannot compete with the fact that Christians have a God who knows the way out of a grave. Not only has God faced up to death, but he has remained loyal through it.

It is different because it has a God who has faced up to poverty. A church has welcomers; a shopping mall has security guards. So where are the poor going to be embraced? It is the Christian God who has announced himself to be good news for the poor. But more than that, he has demonstrated his commitment to the poor by emptying himself of the riches of heaven and living among them. All that money can buy is useless to those who are rejected because they cannot afford to worship in the consumers' temple. Not only has God faced up to poverty, but he has remained loyal through it.

It is different because it has a God who has faced up to weakness. The goods available to those with money to spend announce themselves through images of mythologically perfect and slender young women; through photographs of nakedly unblemished and muscular young men. This, they declare, is what we must strive to be. But the salvation of humankind announces itself with the image of a scorned and helpless victim on the verge of an undeserved death. This, it declares, is all you need to encounter heaven. You don't have to be strong or clever or beautiful or skilful. You just have to be dead. Jesus will do the rest. He already has. Not only has God faced up to weakness, but he has remained loyal through it.

When St Paul was trying to capture the nature of God's loyalty, he referred to a hymn which seems to have been well known in the years after Jesus' resurrection:

> Here is a trustworthy saying:
> If we died with him, we will also live with him;
> if we endure, we will also reign with him.
> If we disown him, he will also disown us;
> But if we are faithless, he will remain faithful,
> for he cannot disown himself.[6]

These are the facts as they have been passed down to us, and that is the reason countless millions devote their loyalty to a God who offers no guarantees, no discount vouchers, no special offers and no quick solutions.

He may lead me on paths that are not safe; he may separate me from those I love; he may take me to places where I recognize nothing. But he remains faithful, and therefore I will trust him.

He may make me confused; make my spirit weary; fill me with apprehension at what the future holds. But he remains faithful, and therefore I will trust him.

He may lead me to question all the things I used to be sure of; he may give me every indication of his plan for me then lead me abruptly to a closed door; he may put me through events whose significance will be a mystery until the very day I reach heaven. But he remains faithful, and therefore I will trust him.

I have no idea how or whether such loyalty will be rewarded when we meet God in the place where all can 'come, buy and eat, without money and without cost'.[7] But I'm on my way to find out!

Notes

1 The Royal Society for the Encouragement of Arts, Manufactures and Commerce (RSA), 16 January 2001.
2 2 Timothy 1:7.
3 Linda Jones and Rebecca Dudley (eds), *Turn the Tables*, Cafod, 2003.
4 Psalm 78:35–37.
5 Psalm 78:38–39.
6 2 Timothy 2:11–13.
7 Isaiah 55:1.

4

Bottled Water

Snapshot: I am in Edinburgh. I am at a bus stop talking to Suzanne, who is on her way to a club. She is wearing a pale blue, cropped top which reveals her midriff, and the jeans that perch on her hips are skin-tight to the knee and then flared to the ground – as if the 1980s and 1970s reached a truce after a fashion war. We have fallen into conversation because I have rescued the water bottle that she dropped. Evian is her water of choice, and she sucks soberly on the nipple-shaped top: 'I think Evian is probably more pure than the others. And it is hundreds of times purer than tap water. You just have to look at the label. I have never wanted to put chemicals in my body, ever since I was young. I can't think of any of my friends who don't carry a bottle of water. Girls anyway! It calms you down when the pace of life gets too much.'

Suzanne is thirteen!

Snapshot: I am in Paris. In Colette's Water Bar there are over eighty bottled waters on offer. They are described with all the precision of a wine list – 'sparkling' and 'still' replacing 'white' and 'red'. Colette's is a basement bar with an ice-cool, minimalist design beneath a row of expensive clothes shops. I give up on the menu and choose entirely on the basis of the shape of the bottle. When I confess to this, the waiter assures me that most customers do the same unless they have an interest in water from a particular country. It is here that I realize how strongly France dominates the market for bottled water. French adults drink an average of eighty litres of bottled water every year (about six times the British average, although sales in Britain have risen 20 per cent per year since the turn of the century). It is part of French heritage. In AD 363 the short-lived Roman Emperor Jovian stopped at Evians-les-Bains, beside Lake Geneva, to taste the Evian water on his way to Germany to preach Christian tolerance. But even before that, in AD 218, Hannibal made a detour to Perrier, in the south of France, because he had heard that the waters would revive his victorious but battle-weary troops.

The water in the glittering, bronze teardrop of a bottle that I have chosen turns out to come from Wales!

Snapshot: I am in Sri Lanka. I am being extremely careful about what I drink. I am even brushing my teeth in bottled water. Around the table in the restaurant are inspirational people who run organizations to improve the lives of Sri Lanka's poorest communities. Among them is Ranjith da Silva, whose model farm is a training centre where hundreds of families have learnt organic techniques that have dramatically increased the yield of their plots, and thus the quality of their lives.[1] I ask the waiter to bring water, but he brings a jug of tap water so I ask for a bottle instead. I fill up everyone's glass, but Ranjith declines and reaches for the jug: 'I do not believe I should have to pay for something that God sends every human being out of the sky.' I think I may have offended him. The curry is hot enough to thaw an igloo, but I can't bring myself to drink another drop. I smuggle the half-empty bottle back to my hotel room.

The water is labelled Hethersett Mountain Springs. It comes from a spring on the Hethersett tea estate, which was founded in 1879 by William Flowerdew from the Norfolk town of Hethersett. The label explains:

The water in this bottle has been drawn from springs originating at the highest elevations in Sri Lanka and processed in the cool mountains where the elevation is nearly 7000 feet above sea level. It is located amidst the lush tea plantations that produce the world's finest teas. This spring water has not been treated with chemicals. It goes through a thorough state-of-the-art process of filtration as well as exposure to ultra violet rays which ensure elimination of bacterial and viral organisms ... It is well within the standards laid down by the World Health Organisation. Best before 30 June 2003.

Sri Lanka is smaller than Ireland, has endured twenty years of civil war, and is home to some of the most poorly paid people of the world, but nevertheless produces over fifty brands of bottled water. There is local controversy over whether the purity claimed by some of them lives up to the photographs of mountain waterfalls on the labels. An investigation by a national newspaper found only two samples (of which Hethersett was one) that measured nil for all types of coliform bacteria, and argued for compulsory national standards.[2]

The following day a car takes me all 7,000 feet up to the Eyerie tea estate. The tea bushes stretch in bright green lines across the steeps as if they had been combed for inspection. Tea pluckers bend between the rows. I climb down the side of the hill to one of the villages – steep, irregular steps in the rock. The two-roomed houses are in rows of three or four, shelved down the side of the mountain. There are window frames but no glass; cables but no electricity; chairs but no cushions. Outside each group of houses is a dust path with a dauntingly basic outside toilet. The generosity of the family I visit is overwhelming.

In the sunshine, the brook that tumbles down the

mountain is flashing diamonds of light into the morning. It has been diverted and piped through a chute so that the water spurts into a pool at the end of the lane. Under the cascade, clothes are washed, children shower, and kettles are filled to make sweet, creamy tea for the visitors. Dazzled by the sparkle of the pure mountain spring I cup my hands and gulp down scintillating mouthfuls of bubbling refreshment.

Like hell I did! I clung on to my bottle of Hethersett mineral water as if one drip from the stream would poison me.

But it was on the Eyerie tea estate that the ironies of bottled water became most apparent. Bottled water is sold by appealing to the notions of 'purity' which are represented by the same mountain streams that would have been so unwise to drink from without first boiling the water. And labels on the bottle show photographs taken in mountain villages where the household income is about 80 pence per day – not enough to buy a litre once it has been filtered, treated, packaged and put on the shelf of a shop. The population of the UK drinks about 1.2 billion litres of bottled water per year, matching uncomfortably the figure of 1.2 billion people world-wide who still have no access to clean drinking water.

In 1970 there were over one hundred projects in operation that had the aim of providing clean water for every human on the planet by the end of the twentieth century – a vision that did not seem unreasonable at the time. But at the beginning of this century, twenty-six countries are thought to have a moderate to severe water shortage, and that is expected to rise to sixty-six by 2050. Demand is dramatically outstripping supply, with consumption of water rising at twice the rate of the population – the main demand being for use in agriculture and industry. For example Lake Chad, which supplies water for six central

African countries, has shrunk by 95 per cent since 1960 but it will need to serve 50 per cent more people by the middle of the century.[3]

It is difficult to come to terms with these facts when we live on a planet nearly three-quarters of which is covered by water. However, the reality is that 97 per cent of that is salt water. Of the rest, nearly 70 per cent is frozen in the ice caps of Antarctica and Greenland, and much of the remainder is at present inaccessible to humans because it is present as soil moisture or deep underground. Less than 1 per cent of the world's fresh water is accessible for human use. Ideas for how to harvest that water, which might once have seemed to belong to science fiction, are now actively being investigated. Scientists at the University of Chile are working on cost-effective methods of harvesting clouds by collecting coastal fog in huge polypropylene nets that trap and condense the water vapour. And the suggestion that icebergs could be towed south seems to be changing from a joke to a research topic. All this is taking place in the context of rising anxieties that access to water might drive nations to war during this century with the same urgency that access to oil did in the last. Observers of the Middle East, where the need to secure sufficient clean water to sustain the population has been a pressing issue for thousands of years, watch with anxiety as deep arterial wells built by Israel monopolize the underground water supply, leaving Palestinian farmers in the Gaza Strip embittered as they are forced to learn desalination techniques and alternative technologies to store and disseminate rainfall.[4] In October 2002 Israel made military threats against Lebanon relating to access to the Wazzani Spring, exacerbating tensions in an area that has long been charged with potential for conflict.

In the face of these forbidding facts (or perhaps because

of them) the market for bottled water grows and grows, and the contrast increases between the way the relatively wealthy enjoy their drinking water and the thirst of the relatively poor to have a safe supply.

And tastes change too. Twenty years ago sparkling water accounted for three-quarters of sales of bottled water in the UK, but sales of still water have now overtaken the carbonated variety. The luxury, fizzy drink is being outsold by the basic, staple tap-water substitute. The largest increase has been in sales of five-gallon containers of water to workplaces for use in water coolers. And the most noticeable development has been the replacement of glass for packaging with polyethylene terephthalate (PET) because of improvements in technology which have eliminated the risk of the water assimilating the taste of the plastic.

Alongside this, variations on the basic product multiply. Under strictly drawn-up regulations, drinking water must be sugar-free and calorie-free, but it may still be called water if flavours (fruits or spices) are added, provided that the additives are clearly labelled and constitute less than 1 per cent of the weight. Beverages with a greater proportion are classified as soft drinks, to be sold alongside lemonade or Coca Cola. Sparkling water is defined by the quantity of carbon dioxide that bubbles to the surface when the bottle is opened. They may not necessarily be the same bubbles that were originally in the spring, because often the water is filtered and the carbon dioxide replaced, but the amount of gas that is added must be the same as the amount that came from the source.

In research in the UK, most consumers suggest that their main reason for buying bottled water is as an alternative to tap water (although figures from the government body which oversees drinking water, the UK Drinking Water Inspectorate, show that it has also taken a swig away from the market share of sugary drinks). Scares over the safety of food during the past ten years and greater knowledge of waterborne organisms which can cause disease (such as cryptosporidium) have both influenced consumer attitudes. Many people perceive bottled water to have a better taste than tap water (the taste of chlorine is a particular dislike). Mineral water, because it is untreated and rich in minerals, is viewed as 'natural', and thus safer and better quality. And its marketing has consistently proposed that drinking bottled water represents a rise on the social scale.

However the Drinking Water Inspectorate suggests that the quality of water from an ordinary tap can be as high or higher than water in a bottle. They point out, for example, that the mineral content from which mineral water gets is name can be extremely variable, and that careful attention to the information on the label of the bottle is needed. In the London area the quantity of calcium and magnesium in ordinary tap water can be higher than in some bottled waters. However, they acknowledge that perceptions are harder to change than facts, and suggest that now that schools are becoming increasingly aware that drinking plenty of water improves children's ability to learn, they should encourage children to drink more by supplying tap water in attractive containers, such as the ones used by athletes, instead of drinking fountains.[5]

The World Wide Fund for Nature goes further by suggesting that drinking mineral water has become 'a trivial habit in many people's lives'. Trivial but not negligible – bottled water costs between 500 and 1,000 times the price of tap water! While acknowledging the need for bottled water in places where the supply is contaminated, the charity draws attention to the 'negative impact on the environment, mainly through fuel combustion'. It points out that water – as bulky as it is cheap – is being transported round the world in bottles that weigh as much as the product inside, using energy that fuels the very climate change which is threatening the world's water resources.[6]

That is the irony of the desire for pure, unspoilt water. Philip Ball, in his book *H2O, a Biography of Water*, begins to make a connection between water and a spiritual search:

> Wherever water is held sacred, the idea of purity manifests itself. Our social attitudes towards pollution and contamination hearken more to the mythic associations of purity than to considerations of natural science. 'Pure' water does not, to most of us, mean water free from all substances that are not H_2O – you can buy such stuff, but only as an expensive fine chemical, not in clear plastic bottles at the supermarket. Rather, we cherish our 'pure' spring water for its very impurities, for the health-giving mineral salts proudly listed on the label . . . I suspect that producers of bottled water understand the mythical dimension of water purity only vaguely, but nonetheless have a strong sense of its selling power.[7]

Philip Ball goes on to describe books that 'invoke the ancient idea that befouled water is cursed.' The Jews of Jesus' day, never having heard of gravity, did not believe that water flowed along its winding route for a scientific reason. They thought that water took its course because God willed it that way. So when they built cisterns, complicated principles were used in their construction to ensure that, for the most holy purposes at least, the water still flowed in its natural direction. They called water with these qualities 'living water'. Israel was an occupied nation under a Roman government that was responsible for the well-being of its citizens. The authorities saw the need to ensure the health of their subjects, both the Jews and the Roman settlers, so they built mighty aqueducts in order to bring clean water to those who lived in the cities. They were bewildered when righteous Jews found this to be a problem. The Jews' religious belief was that the water had been contaminated – it was 'bloody water'. So compelling was the concept that water which sprang naturally from the ground was pure (both in a religious sense and a health-giving sense) that they rejected the better quality water which the government had organized to be brought to them. Their message to Roman officialdom was, 'We don't want your bloody water,' which is disconcertingly similar to the message that consumers in the UK are sending to their local Water Boards!

When Jesus began his ministry he sought out John the Baptist in the remote countryside, where he was offering baptism in the living waters of the River Jordan. Those who wanted their lives to flow in a godly direction, said Jesus, should put their trust in him as the means by which the Spirit of God would stream into their lives: 'If anyone is thirsty, let him come to me and drink. Whoever believes in me . . . streams of living water will flow from within.'[8]

In Jewish thinking the need for pure water for physical health had long been associated with a need for moral or spiritual purity. After their escape from Egypt it took the Israelites only three days to realize that their journey through the wilderness toward the Promised Land would be a precarious one because of the constant search for water. Initial relief at finding an oasis fomented into anger when the water was discovered to be too contaminated to drink. They named the site Marah, which sounds like the Hebrew word for bitter, reflecting both their mood and the impurity of the spring. Their leader Moses responded by treating the water with wood from a nearby tree – either a miraculous intervention of God or a primitive filtering device. The result was that the water became drinkable. But the lesson the Israelites were called to learn was that health would come by adhering obediently to the commands of God: 'If you listen carefully to the voice of the Lord your God and do what is right in his eyes . . . I will not bring on you any of the diseases I brought on the Egyptians, for I am the Lord, who heals you.'[9] Purity of water and purity of lifestyle were permanently coupled.

The Jewish and Christian writings are, however, distinct from those of nearly all other religious traditions in refusing to venerate natural phenomena such as springs. There are no water gods or sacred rivers such as the ones that appear in Hindu or Babylonian mythology. Living creatures are not created out of water, as they are in the Koran. Instead, the beginning of the Bible portrays God as separate from the waters – both have existed eternally. The Spirit of God broods above them, transforming something forbidding and formless into a place pregnant with life.[10] The entire sweep of the Bible shows the progress of the created order to be from dark, sterile water before the era of material existence to the living waters of heaven, flowing as a life-giving river through a city in which there is permanent light.[11] And it is suggested that the purpose of human existence is to develop a context in which water is redeemed and made pure for the eternal life of humankind. Clean water freely available to all, banishing thirst. Salt water driven out of existence, banishing tears:

> Never again will they hunger;
> never again will they thirst.
> The sun will not beat upon them,
> nor any scorching heat.
> For the Lamb at the centre of the throne will be their
>   shepherd;
> he will lead them to springs of living water.
> And God will wipe away every tear from their eyes.[12]

As if to echo that reclamation of water for the healing purposes of God, Christians have historically transformed pagan places into centres of pilgrimage in which the worship of Jesus Christ was central. In fact San Pellegrino, the Italian spa town where waters are bottled for the well-known brand which is part of the Perrier group, actually means 'pilgrim'.

The spring waters of Bath were bubbling out of the Somerset earth at a temperature of 46°C long before England was inhabited, and were evidently in use some seven thousand years ago. The Celts decided that such a wonder was clearly the work of a divine hand and dedicated a shrine beside the spring to the god Sulis. The Romans reclaimed the waters for their own deities and built a temple beside it to Minerva, the goddess of wisdom. So the spring already had a long history as a place of religious healing when the Christians arrived. Rather than declare such associations to be pagan and sinful, they appropriated them for Jesus Christ. They built a hospital on the site, a centre for both spiritual and medicinal healing, and dedicated it (fittingly) to John the Baptist.

One thousand years before John baptized Jesus, King David was at war against the Philistines. It was the latest in a series of wars fought by David in which (with chilling echoes of today's Middle East conflict) command of the water source was crucial. To conquer Jerusalem he had exploited a weak point in the water supply[13] and in Rabbah his armies had defeated the Ammonites (from present-day Jordan) by seizing control of the springs.[14] But in battle against the Philistines David found himself taking shelter in a cave overlooking a valley in which the enemy forces were encamped. Thirsty and war-weary, David slumped into melancholy with the knowledge that Bethlehem, his birthplace, was in enemy hands. With a sigh that resonated with nostalgia for the innocence of his young life he murmured, 'Oh, if only I could hold in my hands a cup of pure water from the well at the gate of Bethlehem!'

Three of David's élite troop, at extreme personal risk, broke through enemy lines. They fought their way into Bethlehem, fetched water from the well, made their perilous way back to David's base, and presented it to him – living water in a dry land. Hearing their story and realizing the great esteem in which he was held by his men, David was deeply moved: 'This water is too pure for me to drink, for it is as precious as the blood of the soldiers who risked their lives for me. It shall not be for me; it shall be for the Lord.' And he lifted the water before God as an act of worship and poured it out of the bowl into the dust.[15]

Snapshot: I am in South London. I am standing next to the font in which my godson is being baptized. It is a breath-freezing winter morning and the low sun is beaming almost horizontally through the church window. It shines so intensely on the trickling water that it seems as if Billy is being baptized in light. I am suddenly and unexpectedly emotional. I want the whole of his life to be as pure and sparkling and still as this moment, but I know that is impossible. As I feel tears threatening my eyes I realize why water, vital and elemental, is the perfect symbol for the beginning of a life of faith. 'It shall be for the Lord.' So while I make my vows on his behalf I am praying that Billy will find for himself a life which is not distracted by eye-catching packaging or alluring marketing, but that he will find himself drawn to the living waters that flow as God wills them. Just as Jesus was for his own baptism into all the laughter and hurt and reality of being human.

As I arrive at the party following the church service I am offered a glass of rather splendid wine, but for reasons

which are known only to me (and now to you) I decline it
and take my glass to the tap.

Notes

1 The Gami Seva Sevana centre, Galaha, Sri Lanka.
2 *The Sunday Times*, Sri Lanka, 23 June 2002.
3 Figures from www.worldwatercouncil.org, and
   www.tearfund.org
4 www.pal-arc.org, the website of the Palestinian Agricultural
   Relief Committees.
5 *Drinking Water 2001*, a report by Michael Rouse, the Chief
   Inspector of the Drinking Water Inspectorate, July 2002.
6 Catherine Ferrier, *Bottled Water: Understanding a Social
   Phenomenon*, WWF, April 2001.
7 Philip Ball, *H2O, a Biography of Water*, Weidenfeld &
   Nicolson, 1999.
8 John 7:37, 38.
9 Exodus 15:22–26.
10 Genesis 1:1–3.
11 Revelation 22:1, 2, 5.
12 Revelation 7:16, 17.
13 2 Samuel 5:8.
14 2 Samuel 12:27.
15 2 Samuel 23:13–17.

5

The Swoosh

In the year 393 the Roman Emperor Valentinian II was murdered. His usurper Eugenius was determined to be rid of the upstart Christian faith and restore paganism to the empire. There was a battle of wills and ideologies. At its heart was an altar to Nike, the winged Goddess of Victory, which Valentinian had ordered to be removed from the Senate House.[1] The pagans demanded the return of the altar to Nike because they thought that its removal from the heart of power had undermined the Roman Empire. They feared that their world-wide domination would lose its inspiration if they lost its symbol. However, under Bishop Ambrose of Milan Christianity was winning hearts and minds by championing another way altogether. Ambrose, in both his life and his teaching, advocated humility and improvement of the circumstances of the poor. It was the Christians who prevailed. The altar was never rebuilt.

On the peak of the baseball cap which has faithfully hidden my hairline for ten years on its long journey north is embroidered a rounded, wing-like tick which swooshes energetically from left to right.

Nike.

Has it come to this?

The Swoosh logo was devised in 1971. The chief executive of Nike, Phil Knight, began selling athletic shoes in the USA in the 1960s and had a substantial business success because jogging had become the keep-fit craze of North America's sunnier states. Jogging as a middle-class fad ran out of pace, to be succeeded by aerobics. The rival company Reebok, which produced trendy indoor aerobic shoes, was beginning to dominate the market. Looking for a design that would give Nike shoes an aesthetic advantage, Phil Knight approached Caroline Davidson, whom he had met at Portland State University where he was teaching accountancy and she was studying design. She had a particular interest in advertising, so the concept of a symbol that could be used both to decorate and promote a product intrigued her. She was asked to create a simple image that could be printed on the side of any shoe in the Nike range. The result was the swoosh logo, for which she was paid $35.

Caroline Davidson's design is based on a wing (speed, flight, energy). It is angled so that it resembles a tick (positivity, correctness, affirmation). And it thrusts in an aerodynamic upward sweep from a rounded left to a pointed right (inspiration, motivation, victory). One glance at the statue of the Nike of Samothrace in the Louvre in Paris reveals Davidson's inspiration. The marble figure, two and a half metres high, is considered to be the finest ancient Greek sculpture to have survived. It was discovered on the Aegean island of Samothrace in 1863. It portrays Nike, Goddess of Victory, her wings spread and her robes rippling in the wind, touching down on earth. The head and arms of the statue are missing, which is understandable for a sculpture that was created about two hundred years before the birth of Jesus. Their absence gives even greater prominence to the wings, the triumphant upward curve of which is mirrored in the swoosh.

Phil Knight made a decision that Nike would diversify into a company which provided every kind of clothing that was required for sports and fitness – all embellished with the swoosh. The legend is that the founders of the company were sport fanatics who hero-worshipped the USA's finest athletes. A more cynical analysis is that they were shrewd businessmen who recognized that there was a small group of sportsmen who could be turned into superstars possessing the same aura that surrounded Hollywood idols. They took on the sporting establishment, which still clung on to an idealism about the nature of sport that distinguished between amateurism (which was noble and classic) and professionalism (which was tainted by financial gain). By offering large sums of money to athletes to choose to wear Nike garments when they competed (the legality of which was always controversial) they created a group of sports men and women who were prepared to stand up against what were portrayed as the old-fashioned and retrograde rules of sporting conduct. Celebrity endorsements were not new, and logos were not new. However, the way the reputations of athletes and the make of clothes they wore rose dizzyingly together was entirely new. The idea that a particular make of training shoes might, of itself, cause someone who enjoyed a weekend kick-about to aspire to become a champion was revolutionary. In the mid-1980s sportswear companies moved on from selling sports kit on the basis of its usefulness, comfort, or even its look. They began appealing directly to our desire to excel, to be heroic, to triumph. The message was and is that Nike (and subsequently its rivals) could give you something that money cannot buy. And Nike could give it to you for cash or for credit. This was not just advertising; this was branding.

In the 1980s 'the brand' was revolutionizing the way goods for sale were presented to the public. The brand is more than a logo or a catch-phrase through which a product is advertised. It is a calculated attempt to give a company as a whole an identity of ideal characteristics, creating associations in the minds of shoppers between the name of the business (no matter which of their products is in front of them) and inspirational qualities.

It is successful branding which leads people to buy a book published by Mills and Boon even though they have never heard of either the author or the title. They know that it will be romantic, escapist and in good taste. It is successful branding which leads people to buy underwear from Marks and Spencer with confidence. It is associated in their minds with basic reliability, reasonable price and the ease with which clothes can be changed if, four hours later, they don't look as desirable as they did in the shop. These associations do not come about by accident – they are expensively nurtured by research, trials and marketing. Both companies attempted to increase their profits during the 1990s by refining the image of their brand (in both cases by stepping up its sexiness and seeking younger customers), and in neither case was it successful. They have both entered the twenty-first century having returned to what their loyal customers wanted all along, with unmistakable benefits.

Branding is not a new phenomenon. I can remember my mother as long ago as the 1960s forcing my unwilling arms into spectacularly unfashionable sweaters with the words 'It's a good make', by which she meant 'I have heard of the name written on the label'. Disney (family-friendly), Heinz (convenience with variety) and Shell (reliability) were already strongly associated with particular qualities. And even before that, brands were intended to generate emotion. The children who crooned 'We are the Ovaltineys, happy girls and boys' perfectly conveyed the innocent spiritedness which would stir up the nation to survive the Second World War as easily as stirring up a mug of hot, malted milk.

But in the late 1980s new theories of commerce were changing the assumption that the main business of a company was production, with branding as the means by which an item reached the public. Increasingly the brand was becoming the business. Brand awareness had its defining moment in 1988 when the Kraft dairy product corporation, its assets worth about $2 billion, was sold for over six times that figure. The five letters of the word 'Kraft' were calculated to be worth $10 billion world-wide in terms of the heart-warming associations they conveyed to consumers.

And on the crest of these thermal currents flew the swoosh. It has come to symbolize the triumph of the brand over the product. Nike does not produce a single shoe, shirt or short. It owns no factories. What it does is commission, brand and sell. It is a phenomenon, and hundreds of more traditional companies are diligently copying its model. Scott Bedbury was head of marketing at Nike when their slogan 'Just Do It!' was launched, before moving to the multinational coffee-shop chain Starbucks. He writes:

> Nike is leveraging the deep emotional connection that people have with sports and fitness . . . A great brand raises the bar – it adds a greater sense of purpose to the experience, whether it is the challenge to do your best in sports and fitness or the affirmation that the cup of coffee you're drinking really matters.[2]

It is to just such an emotional connection that Nike appeals in its mission statement, framed in almost religious language:

> To bring inspiration and innovation to every athlete* in the world.
> *If you have a body you are an athlete.

The asterisk is a quote from Bill Bowerman. Who is he? Legendary track and field coach at the University of Oregon. A teacher who showed athletes the secrets of achievement. Co-founder of Nike. Husband, father, mentor. From him we derive our mission. Through his eyes we see our future.[3]

Prophecy. Teaching. Discipleship. Mythology. Moral virtuousness. Inclusivity. Human worth. It is the whole Bible in a couple of paragraphs. Who needs the Word?

Not the swoosh! In 1996 the swoosh went textless. That is to say, the brand was considered to have such powerful global recognition that the logo alone conveyed 'Nike' without the need for the word to appear above it on garments. Research had revealed it to be among the most recognizable symbols in the world, rivalling the five Olympic Games rings and McDonald's golden arches in its ability to convey meaning without words. And, of course, the Christian cross!

During 2003, when Nike had become one of the select few companies that does $10 billion of business every year world-wide, the brand hiccoughed. Shares in Nike plunged 21 per cent as customers (particularly in the United States) turned their attention to other, newer labels. It was suggested that having placed so much emphasis on branding and technology, Nike had lost sight of the old-fashioned desire for good design (it is said the Nike Shox basketball shoe, although endorsed by stars and a scientific marvel, is 'a laced-up brick'[4])! Others went further and foresaw problems for the whole concept of branding. Journalist Geraldine Bedell reflects on the realization that 'Brands weren't the answer to everything and sometimes they weren't even necessary: sushi has shot around the world without any branding at all. Customers are involved in much more of a dialogue with brands than was realised a few years ago.'[5]

But the swoosh is fighting back, customizing clothes and creating 'smart' products with features that are computerized to feed into networks. And nobody is suggesting defeat for the Goddess of Victory as long as she continues to inspire worship where angels fear to tread – among the young, black males of urban America. By borrowing style and attitude from the backstreets, and then sponsoring 'charitable' sports programmes in inner cities, Nike has ensured that the swoosh has become a walking advertisement on the hot bodies of cool people. So valuable is the informal promotion of the logo being seen on 'the right people' that Nike has consistently resisted the urge to crack down on the pirating of the swoosh, and has even been accused of turning a blind eye to theft. One of the results of this is that the swoosh is in evidence almost everywhere in the developing world – faked, second-hand, or crudely drawn on clothes – in places where an entire day's wages could not buy a Nike shoelace.

In many tattoo parlours in North America the swoosh has become one of the most requested symbols. Carmine Colettion, a twenty-four-year-old internet entrepreneur has one on his navel: 'I wake up every morning, jump in the shower, look down at the symbol, and that pumps me up for the day. It is to remind me every day what I have to do, which is "Just do it!"'

When your customers want to spend their own money increasing your advertising budget, every dollar you invest in it must seem well spent. In 1997 Nike spent $500 million on advertising (an estimated twenty-fold increase over a decade). Their definitive advertisement was one made in order to sell Air Jordan trainers. In it Michael Jordan, who at the time was without question the most talented basketball player in the world, accelerated across a court until (to the accompaniment of jet engines revving) he soared impossibly through the air toward the hoop. Made in 1985 as pop videos were coming spectacularly into their own, it used the visual language of MTV – freeze frames and jump cuts. It made the Nike training shoe into an icon; it made Michael Jordan into a dream. In fact it is difficult to work out who benefitted more, since Jordan's profile rose so steeply that, during the years in which he has bounced between retirements and comebacks, he has become a brand in his own right. Within the Nike empire he has his own clothing line, not just basketball kit but also leisure wear, showcased in a chain of shops across the USA.

In 2002 John Schultz directed a film called *Like Mike*. In it the forlorn and diminutive underdog of a Dickensian orphanage, played by the teenage actor Lil' Bow Wow (I'm not making this up!) finds a pair of trainers with the initials MJ inside. Imagining them to be cast-offs of Michael Jordan, he discovers that when he wears them and whispers, 'Make me like Mike,' he develops a championship-winning basketball talent. Anyone who failed to make the leap through the alphabet from Like to Mike to Nike was helped on his way by constant product placement. The fact that comments about the film ranged from 'deeply flawed' to 'deeply disappointing' is irrelevant. It was deeply swooshed!

In April 2003 Nike had a new hero to laud. It signed a five-year sponsorship deal for $90 million with all 6 feet 8 inches of the eighteen-year-old basketball prodigy LeBron James. The campaigner Ralph Nader[7] sent an open letter to the young man explaining to him the controversies that surround the making of Nike clothes and asking him to use some of his new resources and influence to support justice for those who make them. LeBron James was brought up in a deprived area of Akron, Ohio, by a teenage mother while his father was in prison. He seemed to have other things on his mind. His response to the contract was: 'When I was younger I didn't have much. And now that I have got a little something I'm just gonna take it.' In the same year a factory worker in Indonesia making Nike shoes, six days a week, 10¼ hours a day, could typically earn $864 in a year (just over two dollars per day).[8] An Indonesian factory worker could expect to equal the athlete's wage packet in 20,833 years.

Research by Oxfam Community Aid Abroad reveals that the greatest concern of workers is that they have been forced to leave their children behind in their home villages and migrate in order to seek work in the factories. They do not earn enough to keep their children with them so they see them only once per month, or less often if home is more than two hundred miles away.[9] Naomi Klein's eye-opening book, *No Logo*, tells the story of the rise and rise of branding and draws attention to inadequacies in the working conditions of employees working in Chinese factories. Among others, the book draws attention to the Yeun Yeun factory where athletic shoes are produced for both Nike and Adidas. Workers put in between sixty and eighty-four hours per week for $0.19 per hour. The sources quoted allege forced overtime with no premium, excessive fumes and noise, and that no employee had heard that there is a Nike corporate code of conduct.[10]

The code of conduct was established in January 1992 in response to international pressure on transnational corporations to take responsibility for the well-being of the employees in the factories that are contracted to make their products. Nike requires it to be displayed in full in the factory and given in summary to every worker. It covers respect of the rights of employees (including freedom from discrimination, corporal punishment, forced labour or child labour), safety and health in the workplace, and minimizing the negative impact on the environment.

And is the code effective? Nike insists that it is. No Sweat, the organization that campaigns against sweatshops worldwide, is in doubt. Mick Duncan, its national secretary, says, 'If they're cleaning up their act, how come they are happy to pull the plug on factories where increased wages and decent living conditions have been won? If they're really only interested in working with subcontractors who use a unionised work force, how come they are moving so much production to China where you are lucky if you only go to prison for being a member of a union? And . . .' (a grin crosses his face) 'how come I got chucked out of the Nike Town shop at Oxford Circus for giving out information?'

No Sweat is encouraged by what it sees as campaign successes and in 2003 hosted a conference with keynote speakers from Mexico City where union leaders had negotiated a significant pay and conditions deal in a factory: 'It is exciting stuff. Nike wanted to pull out after the increase in labour costs but they've been forced not to . . . I'm not religious. I just hate injustice. I have always hated injustice and I wanted to do something about it. For me that is what it is all about, so we try to do what we can.'[11]

Religious or not, Mick Duncan's attitude echoes the words that Old Testament prophets put in the mouth of God. In the Bible, the behaviour that God demands is:

> To loose the bonds of injustice,
> to undo the thongs of the yoke,
> to let the oppressed go free,
> and to break every yoke.[12]

The prophets of the Old Testament attributed the catastrophes which Israel faced to God turning a deaf ear to their prayers because the enthusiastic worship of the people was not matched by lives in which the vulnerable were protected and the poor helped. The accusations which No Sweat levels at clothing brands are all present in the equally outspoken denunciation of the people of Israel by the shepherd-turned-activist Amos eight hundred years before Jesus. He points to frustration at having to give workers a day of rest because it stops every last penny of profit being squeezed, and of a 'race to the bottom' to get the maximum return from the smallest outlay no matter what the human cost may be:

> Hear this, you that trample on the needy
> and bring to ruin the poor of the land,
> saying, 'When will the new moon be over so that we may
>   sell grain;
> and the sabbath, so that we may offer wheat for sale?
> We will make the ephah small and the shekel great,
> and practice deceit with false balances,
> buying the poor for silver
> and the needy for a pair of sandals,
> and selling the sweepings with the wheat.'[13]

The ephah was a large vessel used to measure out corn for a shopper. The shekel was used to weigh out the silver with which he paid for it. By making the ephah small and the shekel great a crooked trader was selling less than he promised for more than he agreed. Today the problem has been reversed – it is the powerful companies of the rich nations who can demand more and more of a product for less and less money. The balances have tipped the other way, but the potential for injustice still yawns. Why do poor people agree to work in such punishing conditions in eighth-century BC Israel or twenty-first-century Indonesia?

Because when you have no shoes on your feet, desperation for a pair of sandals can leave you with no choice.

The development charity Christian Aid is one of several organizations which have come together as a Trade Justice Movement campaigning for new rules of international trade that cover both governments and large transnational companies. It insists that trade rules should be enforced so that they benefit not only rich countries that are well positioned to capitalize on their rights, but poor countries as well. And it seeks to change the way in which largely-unregulated transnational corporations operate so that there are legally-binding agreements which work in favour of poor people at the same time as they bring benefits to the lives of rich people.

For Christian Aid Week in 2002 the charity chose for its poster a photograph of a child from a fishing village in Ghana. It has a reputation for choosing positive, industrious images from the developing world that defy stereotypes and use eye contact to create an acknowledgement of shared humanity. However, on this occasion it selected a shot in which the young boy's face is completely obscured by the swoosh on his baseball cap. The fishing net which he has in his hands is totally empty, and the caption asks: 'International trade: where's the catch?' Interestingly, the charity has sufficient confidence in the recognition of its own brand to identify itself on the poster not by the name Christian Aid but by the red door-to-door collecting envelope with which it has been associated for half a century as it opposes global injustice.

Three thousand miles north of Ghana on a street in South London sixteen-year-old Jon Fisk's clothes bear an almost identical swoosh, although they were bought expensively in a shopping mall, not on a market stall of forgeries in the African heat. He has a beige sweater, a blue jacket, black and grey trainers, and a gold chain round his neck, all with Nike's unmistakable logo: 'Yeah, I wear lots of Nike clothes because they're wicked. They bring you confidence. I know it is a false confidence, but it counts because all the kids have the same. It makes you part of a world-wide group.'

Does that go for all labels, or particularly for Nike? 'Mainly Nike. Other brands give you the same respect when they are new, like McKenzie or Diadora, but that is only for a limited time. With Nike you know you are going to stay acceptable, funky . . . long-term sexually promotionable [*sic*].'

When you choose your clothes, who do you want to look like? 'David Beckham, Eminem, Tim Henman . . . errr . . . half of Croydon, so that you can fit in with all different kinds of people. I like the fact that it makes you look intimidating, which gives you a certain power. I feel a bit guilty about wanting to have power, but at the end of the day I need that because I want to be liked for who I am.'

And of course, that is what we would all like! The desire for a sense of personal worth is central to the development of an inner life that is unique to human beings. In different ways there is a longing within us all to be inspired, to have experiences and feelings which touch our souls. It is a basic human desire 'to have life, and have it to the full', whether or not we are aware that this fulfilment is precisely what Jesus claimed to bring to the human condition through his love, intimate and individual knowledge, and compassionate sacrifice.[14] Although church leaders may be disappointed by the way in way in which they seek it, young people wear Nike clothes because they aspire to the very same spiritual fulfilment which the Christian faith holds out to them. Love and power! These are age-old yearnings as we search for self-esteem. Those who seek them in the swoosh are addressing the needs of the same inner being that Paul believed Jesus could enrich, and about which he wrote to a small church surrounded by potent anti-Christian interests in Ephesus:

> I pray that out of his glorious riches [God] may strengthen you with power through his Spirit in your inner being, so that Christ may dwell in your hearts through faith. And I pray that you, being rooted and established in love, may have power, together with all the saints, to grasp how wide and long and high and deep is the love of Christ.[15]

In her compelling analysis of how the brand has become such a dominant force despite persistent questions about the human cost of that force, Naomi Klein writes:

> That 'deep inner need' for designer gear has grown so intense that it has confounded everyone from community leaders to the police. Everyone pretty much agrees that brands like Nike are playing a powerful surrogate role in the ghetto, subbing for everything from self-esteem to African-American cultural history to political power. What they are far less sure about is how to fill that need with empowerment and a sense of self-worth that does not necessarily come with a logo attached . . . In its press material and ads, there is an almost messianic quality to Nike's portrayal of its role in the inner cities: troubled kids will have higher self-esteem, fewer unwanted pregnancies and more ambition – all because at Nike, 'We see them as athletes'. For Nike its $150 Air Jordans are not a shoe but a kind of talisman with which poor kids can run out of the ghetto and better their lives. Nike's magic slippers will help them fly.[16]

Like Mike!

The anti-Nike campaign is the most sustained of any against a multinational business, and it claims successes. In 1997 Nike agreed to sign the Fair Labour Association voluntary workplace code of conduct. In the summer of 2001, perhaps in an attempt to laugh off the tarnish on its image, Nike planned an advertising campaign for its Australian football boots with the slogan 'Our most offensive boot yet: 100% slave labour'. It was withdrawn under an onslaught of protest. In the Bronx, Manhattan, social worker Mike Gitelson started to tell young people about the poor pay and conditions of workers in Indonesia which mean that it costs Nike only $5 to make a pair of trainers, and that one of the reasons why their parents found it difficult to get work was that factories in the United States had been forced to close because Nike no longer made any of its shoes there: 'Yo dude, you're being suckered if you pay $100 for a sneaker that costs $5 to make. If somebody did that to you on the block, you know where it's going.'[17] When hundreds of letters written by the young people received identical replies from Nike, they were infuriated that their views had not been taken seriously and planned direct action. They gathered hundreds of pairs of out-of-fashion Nikes that they had stopped wearing and dumped them outside Nike Town. Nike executives immediately responded because, Mike Gitelson surmises, polite middle-class protesters could do the swoosh no harm at all but a backlash growing out of the inner cities would do serious damage.

All of which, curiously, takes us back to Ambrose of Milan in the fourth century. One of the many ways in which he was remarkable is that he led the first recorded direct action protest by Christians. The mother of the Emperor Valentinian wanted to take over one of the churches of

Milan for Arianism (a cult that saw Jesus as a human selected by God for deity). Ambrose opposed it by leading the congregation into the church building, where they sat down and refused to move. They defiantly sang hymns (hymn-singing is another Christian tradition for which we have Ambrose to thank) until they won their building back for orthodox Christian worship.

'Riches are the beginning of all vices, because they make us capable of carrying out even our most vicious desires,' wrote Ambrose, pleading for those with economic might to recognize the moral responsibility they bore for the well-being of those over whom they exercised power. But the battle he fought on behalf of the way of humility and compassion against the belligerence of the Goddess Nike may be more difficult to win this time round because the people she wants to conquer are not resisting.

'You have been rubbed in oil like an athlete, Christ's athlete, as though dressed for an earthly wrestling match, and you have agreed to take on your opponent.'[18] Well there you go! We are all athletes after all!

Notes

1 'Nike' is the Greek name for the Roman goddess known in Latin as 'Victoria'.

2 Quoted in Tom Peters, 'What Great Brands Do', *Fast Company*, August 1997.

3 www.nike.com/nikebiz

4 'The Changing Face of the Brand', *The Observer*, 19 January 2003.

5 Ibid.

6 Quoted in Naomi Klein, *No Logo*, HarperCollins, 2000.

7 Press release of The League of Fans, 8 April 2003.

8 The minimum wage in Indonesia was raised in 2003 to between 350,000 and 790,000 rupiahs per month, depending

on regional variations. In Jakarta the minimum wage was 592,000 rupiahs (about £44). Nike claims to pay just above the minimum wage, but allegations have been made of negotiations for an exemption and threats of a transfer of production to Vietnam.

9 www.caa.org.au/campaigns/nike/faq.html

10 Charles Kerregan, *Company Profiles and Working Conditions: Factories in China Producing Goods for Export to the US*, National Labour Committee, March 1998, quoted in Naomi Klein, *No Logo*.

11 Interviewed by Paul Sharpe for this book, November 2002.

12 Isaiah 58:6.

13 Amos 8:4–6.

14 John 10:10.

15 Ephesians 3:16–18.

16 Naomi Klein, *No Logo*.

17 David Gonzales, 'Youthful Foes go Toe to Toe with Nike', *New York Times*, 27 September 1997.

18 *De Mysteriis* (*On Baptism, Confirmation, and the Blessed Eucharist*), translated by H. de Romestin (Select Library of Nicene and Post-Nicene Fathers, New York, 1896).

6

The Sparrow

I can see one now!

It is the last weekend of January and I am taking part in the Big Garden Birdwatch. It is a national survey in which over a quarter of a million people in the UK are participating. We have all committed ourselves to spend one hour watching our gardens, or a local park, and recording the birds that land during that time. I have a notebook open on my desk and I have called up the website of the Royal Society for the Protection of Birds (which has organized the project) for help with identification of . . . well, let's be honest . . . anything that's not a robin.[1]

Several things are conspiring to frustrate my sole contribution this year to the advancement of science. Apart from breathtaking ignorance, I am also battling against leaden skies, non-stop phone calls and bizarre memories floating unexpectedly back to me across the decades.

I am seventeen. I have been put in charge of the religious content of morning assemblies at school – apparently the fourth person to be asked and the first to realize that the post was being offered as an honour, not a punishment. It is five minutes to nine and the first reluctant worshippers are beginning to file in, when I notice that a sparrow has flown into the hall through a high, open window. He is flying from side to side, not apparently unhappy, but clearly unable to find another window to let him out. A spark of inspiration ignites. I run through the corridors to my locker and reach for a book that I had been using the previous evening for religious education homework. Urged by the teacher in charge to come up with assemblies that are relevant to the day-to-day life of the school, I realize that I have in my hand the reading that will, at long last, draw the attention of the staff to the fact that I am not the annoying little mediocrity they take me to be, but a man of imagination and intelligence. I zip back down the corridors carrying a passage from the Venerable Bede, the seventh-century monk from Jarrow in Northumberland who wrote a history of Christianity in England. I mount the rostrum impressively, and begin to read . . .

> In seems to me that the life of men on earth, in comparison with that time of uncertainty which will eventually come upon us all, is like a winter's night when a king sits feasting with all his noblemen. A single sparrow flies swiftly into the hall and, coming in at one window, instantly flies out through another. During the time in which it is indoors it is not touched by the fury of the winter. And yet, this smallest space of calm is over in a flash. The sparrow passes from winter into winter again, and is lost to human eyes. The life of a man seems a little like this. We are utterly ignorant of what follows or of what went before, and so . . .[2]

I look up from the page, distracted from my reading by swelling noise. Not one single person is listening to me. Their undivided attention is given to the sparrow, which has started to do what sparrows are best known for. Staff are struggling to stifle their laughter; pupils are not bothering to. I try again: 'The life of a man seems . . .' The sparrow launches out again and unleashes a scud missile at one of the least popular boys in the school. A cheer erupts. I admit defeat and step down from the lectern. The head teacher reasserts control by using the last, perfidious resort of an educational tyrant – compulsory hymn singing. The single chance I would ever have of bidding to become a prefect has been scuppered by a sparrow shitting on Charles Bickley of Form 4B.

There's another one!

Actually, I think it is the same sparrow which has come back into my tiny garden for a second visit. For that reason, the figure we have been instructed to record is the largest number of each species we see together in the garden at any one time, not the total number of sightings during the hour. And they need to come right in among the uncontrollable leylandii, not just fly overhead. My results are dismal. I see two starlings, one robin, two blackbirds, three magpies (which will skew the survey because last year's results showed an average of less than one), one grey thing that flew too fast for me to look it up (I'm not sure how helpful that submission is going to be), and one sparrow.[3]

One sparrow! My memories of childhood are that gardens were crammed with sparrows. But Richard Bashford, the coordinator of the event, confirms that my results are not unusual:

> The starling and house sparrow are still likely to be the most numerous species nationally. But in some places very few will be seen . . . It will be notable if someone doing the survey in central London sees more than one or two house sparrows in one spot.[4]

Nobody knows where the sparrows have gone. Their decline is one of the most intriguing mysteries of British wildlife. In the last quarter of a century the UK population has almost halved, from 24 million in the year of my disastrous assembly to less than 14 million. In London the decline is the most shocking – a 75 per cent fall since 1994.[5]

Because no one knows the cause of the house sparrow's decline, no one knows what to do to reverse it. There are many theories. It is certainly true that in past centuries their food supply would have been more secure than it is today, because they were nifty thieves of the corn fed to horses. But explanations for the accelerated downfall are multiplying. A study at Oxford University suggests that changes in winter-time farming practice are the cause – particularly the use of herbicides to control weeds and the bird-proofing of grain stores.[6] German scientists blame gardeners who go to great lengths to annihilate aphids – the greenfly that attack their best plants but are vital for feeding nestling sparrows in their first days.[7] Spanish scientists have discovered that birds avoid places with high levels of electromagnetic charge, and this has led others to point an accusing finger at the mobile-phone mast. It is certainly true that sparrows conti-nue to thrive in the places where the curses of cell phone users about poor reception are heard loudest. Although research is in its early stages and the theories are speculative, scientists are considering the impact of electromagnetic waves both on egg-laying ability and on birds' navigation systems, which rely on the earth's magnetic fields.[8]

And then there is a long list of accusations that are not scientifically documented, but are equally intriguing – loft insulation, rising numbers of grey squirrels, volatile organic compounds in lead-free fuel, attacks by cats which are increasingly likely to be outside during the day because their owners are at work, climate change, and (evidently not having read the warning on the packet) anaphylactic shock from eating peanuts.

A bird that has been commonplace for thousands of years earned its place as a sign of the times when *The Independent* launched a 'Save the Sparrow' campaign with a £5,000 reward for the first convincing reason for the slump in the population of the species. Three hundred explanations later, the prize is unclaimed. And the Royal Society for the Protection of Birds has added the sparrow to its 'Red List' of species whose decline is giving serious cause for concern.

Arthur Ashby, who first twitched his binoculars out of their case and trained them on garden birds over sixty years ago, has his own local explanation: 'In London suburbs their nesting places are disappearing in home improvement schemes. My neighbour had a nest in a cavity in the roof of his house. It was not unusual for me to see families of twelve in the garden. When the roof was rebuilt it was perfect for humans; hopeless for sparrows. They had nowhere to go.'

Arthur tried to explain to me the appeal of bird-watching: 'There is no other area of natural history in which so much that is so interesting comes to your own home. At the bottom of my garden is a holly hedge. It is the boundary of the property and behind it is Gee's Wood. Every year, just before Christmas, fieldfares and redwings fly the length of the hedge on their migratory path. They have done it every year as long as I have lived here, and I imagine they have been doing it for two hundred years. One morning last year, seeing that the bush was spectacularly covered with red berries, I decided that my task later in the day would be to bring some indoors for decoration. By the time I went out in the afternoon to cut it, the fieldfares had swept through and eaten every last berry. They had flown non-stop all the way from Scandinavia. It is not surprising that they decided to take a break for a pub lunch.

'But you can't help loving the sparrows! I am sure they will still be one of the most numerous species in this year's survey, although starlings are more aggressive and may be getting the edge. But the spread of house sparrows will be uneven, with far more sightings in the north-west of England than in the south-east. Last August near Cockermouth I watched two dozen who were dust-bathing together in the summer heat. They like it dirty! And they are such cheeky birds. They thrust their chests out and strut. And the males squabble over the females. It is not a tuneful sound; it is more of a loud chirrup. It is no wonder they used to call kids in the East End of London "cockney sparrows".

'Every one of the explanations for their disappearance relates in some way to the action of humans. I would be very sad if we lose them. I admit that when you look at the world as a whole, losing one species does not seem like a big deal. But there is something undefinable that slips away from us every time a species becomes extinct. Something that is simple and beautiful.'

Gregarious and noisy, chirpy and constantly on the pull, it is hardly surprising that sparrows and humans have been feeding and breeding alongside each other for centuries. As men and women adapted to live in urban and suburban environments, so did *Passer domesticus*. Sparrows are found everywhere from tower block gutters to rural hedgerows. In the male, the black stripe through the eye above white cheeks makes the bird easy to identify. He has dark wings and greyish underparts. The female is duller and browner, with a broad pale band stretching back from her eye.

Their spread across Europe and the Middle East is remarkable. They are recognized in Galashiels and in Galilee. And the irony of their current plight is that almost every reference to them in literature points to a creature that is so populous and commonplace as to be unremarkable. For example, when Jesus drew attention to sparrows (probably the same species) it was to instruct his followers not to worry. And that is why their disappearance is so worrying!

Are not two sparrows sold for a penny? Yet not one of them will fall to the ground apart from the will of your Father. And even the very hairs of your head are all numbered. So don't be afraid; you are worth more than many sparrows.[9]

Appropriately the Old English word for worry, *wyrgan*, was the expression for what a cat would do to a sparrow once it got its teeth into its throat. Not pleasant! When Jesus told his followers not to be afraid it was in the context of sending the twelve to whom he was closest on a mission to the world in his name. And they were to do so with a lifestyle of simplicity. They were to take nothing that would add convenience to their circumstances, let alone luxury. They were to carry no money, but earn what they needed. They were to pack no spare clothes, but make do with what they were wearing. They were to hold lightly to possessions, giving as freely as they received, and relying on the goodness of the earth and its inhabitants. Jesus was not idealistic about the risk or the cost of this way of life. He knew it would mark out his followers as different from those among whom they worked. He was sending them out 'like sheep among wolves'.[10] Or like sparrows among cats!

The fear of the twelve apostles was that of anyone, before or since, who has taken a stand against the predominant culture. It was the fear of being the lone voice – the one person bringing an unpopular message to a culture unwilling to listen, the prophet showing a society the consequences of behaviour that would damage it in time to come. 'The supreme trick of mass insanity,' said the Romanian playwright Eugene Ionesco in an interview, 'is that it persuades you that the only abnormal person is the one who refuses to join in the madness of others, the one who tries vainly to resist.' Such is the role that was freely adopted by Jesus, and the one that his followers have repeatedly found themselves called to imitate, willingly or not.

The reassurance that Jesus offers in those circumstances is that there is no injustice, no injury, no hidden sorrow which is not clearly seen by God. His knowledge is intimate and individual, and the value he puts on the person who is enduring such suffering is unimaginably high.

Sensing himself an isolated voice of righteousness in a government where evil is prevailing, Hamlet refers directly to the words of Jesus, in Shakespeare's play. He has been invited to take part in a demonstration fencing match against his girlfriend's brother, but a foreboding has seized him that the contest has been rigged ('How ill all's here about my heart'). His best friend tries to persuade him to say that he is feeling sick and not up to sword fighting. But Hamlet declares his trust in God. If God knows when the moment of death of every single sparrow will be, then obviously the day of the death of a human cannot be altered from the one that has been ordained. And so every circumstance, no matter how dangerous, can be faced with confidence:

> There's a divinity that shapes our ends, rough-hew them how we will . . . There is a special providence in the fall of a sparrow. If it be now, 'tis not to come; if it be not to come it will be now . . . the readiness is all.[11]

So what happens if we extend Hamlet's view of a world in which God is in complete control of life and death to the circumstances of the planet on which we live at the start of the twenty-first century? What harm does it do us to lose one species, so the argument goes, when countless thousands of species have come and gone under God's control as the millennia have rolled past? The brontosaurus has had its day. Thank God! Why weep for the sparrow?

Professor Paul Ehrlich, of the Centre for Conservation Biology at Stanford University in California, compares species to the rivets that hold an aeroplane together. There is nothing more dispensable than a rivet. A single rivet plays so small a role in the astonishing complexity of a plane that it goes unnoticed. But there is a limit to how many rivets can pop out of your Easyjet no-frills flight to the Mediterranean before the whole structure collapses. Species, says, Paul Ehrlich, are the rivets of Spaceship Earth.

The sparrow is not alone. Of the 9,200 species of birds in the world, over 1,000 are threatened or endangered. And similarly unsettling statistics apply to every other group of living beings that stir or swim or fly or flower or breathe or photosynthesize. But not all of them by any means attract the same affectionate support. Who campaigns on behalf of endangered worms?

John Lawton does. He is the chief executive of the Natural Environment Research Council and was formerly the chair of the RSPB. He records that in June 1990 he watched the last, lone red-backed shrike in England sing with all his might in a Norfolk hedgerow, hopelessly attempting to attract a non-existent female. The sadness he feels is evident in his determination to summon all the resources he can to the aid of endangered species:

> One argument I repeatedly hear is that species are useful, or might be useful, for mankind. That is, they are a potential source of new drugs, new pesticides, new varieties of crops, new genes, new suntan cream, new this and new that. Species are a tool kit, a rummage box of useful gadgets, there to be mined and exploited for our advantage. Therefore we must conserve them.[12]

This is an argument which is often used to persuade politicians that funds allocated to conservation constitute money that urgently needs to be spent. And the result of it is that genetic material from as diverse a range of species as possible is being deep frozen in the form of seeds, sperm and eggs against the future day when it might prove valuable in the progress of human development. The science of this approach is new and high-tech, so it is relatively successful in attracting funding, but John Lawton is disappointed by the thinking that stresses usefulness above all other motives for conservation:

> It is an argument that lacks a soul. It is both sensible and true, but it has no spirit, no human dimension. It is the argument of the technocrats. We do not conserve Mozart concertos, Monet paintings or mediaeval cathedrals because they are useful. We conserve them because they are beautiful and because they enrich our lives. The frozen gene strategy is the conservation equivalent of keeping the architect's drawings for York Minster, whilst levelling the building to make way for a much needed multi-storey car park in the centre of the city; very practical, very useful and totally stupid . . . Nature is beautiful. Let's say so, and let us have the stewardship of that beauty as an honest and major reason for conserving it.[13]

Yes, nature is beautiful. Its beauty is in its fragility. Every individual component of nature comes and goes – lilies fade, flames expire and sparrows die. And yet their essence is constantly being renewed, lily into lily, flame into flame, beauty into beauty. Their glory is the one Bede spoke of – the warm, rich, welcoming beauty of the banqueting hall through which the sparrow flies on its journey from unknown to unknown.

And humankind is beautiful too. Perhaps it is the most precious of all the beautiful things in nature. In choosing to make himself known on earth by inhabiting a human body, God has conferred on humankind a value that is almost inexpressible. But we serve ourselves poorly if we forget that the beauty and value of being human are fragile things too. Why is it that, even while Jesus' reassurance that I am worth far more than any two-a-penny bird is echoing in my ear, I find myself worrying that the whole human species could be Bede's sparrow, enjoying 'the smallest space of calm' between winter and winter?

Only a generation ago the life and landscape of northeast England, where Bede lived and worshipped, was dominated by coal mining. And within living memory, miners kept canaries in cages in the dark, deep underground. Birds are much more sensitive to poisonous gasses than humans. When the canaries died, coal miners knew that something serious was going wrong. They got out quick. The decline of the house sparrow is sending us a warning. But unlike the miners, there is nowhere else for us to go.

Christians have a unique perspective on the environment. They have insights into the winter which is the destiny of all people when they are 'lost to human eyes'. They believe that this beautiful planet Earth does not belong to us. It belongs to Jesus. It was created through him. But even more importantly, it was created for him. In the New Testament, Paul rejoices in this:

> [Jesus Christ] is the image of the invisible God, the first-born over all creation. For by him all things were created: things in heaven and on earth, visible and invisible, whether thrones or powers or rulers or authorities; all things were created by him and for him.[14]

At the end of time, the Bible promises, there will be a

renewed and perfected heaven and earth. All the created order will be presented to Jesus as his own. Then, as the earth returns to the one for whom it was always destined, we will be held accountable for what we have done with it. God forgive us!

And will God forgive us? Of course he will! He forgives again and again, so we are not without hope. Even now it is not too late to turn to him, determined to repent and change. But actions have consequences, even forgiven actions, and we have to live with the results of what we do to our planet.

We must know this. Our children must know this. Our neighbours must know this. Our leaders must know this. In this generation time is not on our side. Let it be clear! This is the last ditch. This is where we turn and fight.

Notes

1 www.rspb.org

2 Bede, *Ecclesiastical History of the English People*, newly translated and abridged from Anglo-Saxon.

3 The results of the survey published in March 2003 revealed starlings to be the most common bird (averaging 4.9 per garden). The house sparrow came second (4.8), followed in order by blue tits (3.1), blackbirds (2.7) and chaffinches (2.2). Sparrows were recorded in 69% of participating gardens. The unidentified grey bird was almost certainly a collared dove, one of the few garden birds whose numbers showed a significant increase.

4 *The Independent*, 25 January 2003.

5 Data from the British Trust for Ornithology.

6 The Edward Grey Institute of Field Ornithology, 2002.

7 *House Sparrows in Hamburg: Population, Habitat Choice and Threats*, Hamburg State Ornithological Protection Station, 2000.

8 *The Observer*, 12 January 2003.

9 Matthew 10:29–31.

10 Matthew 10:16.
11 William Shakespeare, *Hamlet Prince of Denmark*, Act 5, Scene 2.
12 John Lawton, 'Are species useful?', *Oikos, A Journal of Ecology*, Issue 62–1, 1991.
13 Ibid.
14 Colossians 1:15, 16.

7

Spam

Just before Christmas I changed my internet service provider to a brand new company and registered a new e-mail address. Having beaten the queue and applied on the first day, I was delighted to have an easily memorable address – my Christian name, the @ symbol, and the name of the ISP.

Ten days later I received an e-mail unexpectedly. The sender was 'Mary' and the subject line asked, 'How BIG do you want it?' There was a simple explanation – Mary is my mother's name and she was evidently knitting me a sweater. So I opened it.

Even if she had been fully clothed, it would have taken me less than a nano-second to realize that the young woman in the photograph was not my mother. And although I had no previous experience of the activity illustrated, I was reasonably confident that it was unlikely to generate knitwear.

'Spam' is the generic term for electronic mail that arrives uninvited in the inbox of the communication system of a computer, almost always with the intention of selling something. The technical term for it is 'unsolicited bulk e-mail'. But whatever it is called, I am drowning in it!

The mail from 'Mary's' pornographic site multiplied over the next few weeks, and I became adept at recognizing her style in time to delete it before opening. However, one innocuously entitled 'Re: Hello' fooled me into thinking that it was a response to a message I had sent, and so I opened it. Initially revolted, I found a banner that read: 'Click here if you no longer wish to receive e-mails from this address.' I moved the cursor to a rectangular box marked 'Unsubscribe' and sent a polite message asking not to be sent any more unsolicited material.

Oh boy, was that a mistake!

A flood tide of spam followed almost immediately. And now no longer just for pornography, but also for get-rich-quick schemes, suspicious competitions, and music that can be downloaded illegally from a website. The emotion I should have experienced was anger. Instead I persuaded myself that I was guilty. What on earth had I done with my computer for which it was punishing me in this way? I tried to recall all the websites I had visited in case one of them might have inadvertently suggested to a salesman that the owner of my e-mail address had an interest in pornography. I had, admittedly, purchased some underwear by internet, but it was from a well-known commercial site and the garments could not possibly have been less titillating if my mother had hand-knitted them!

It took a visit from a friend whose job is designing websites to ease my conscience. Spam, he assured me, is an evil rain that is sent on both the righteous and the unrighteous. Unless I had been punctilious about ticking the box that protects my personal information every single time I filled in a form, any one of the organizations that had requested my address might have passed it on to a business for it to be sold and resold on CD-roms in batches of millions. The same might be true if I had ever signed up for a competition on-line (yes), posted a message on a discussion board (yes), received an e-mail carbon copied to multiple addresses (yes, many times), or been the victim of a computer virus (yes). And worse still, the fact that my e-mail address was so straightforward and my Christian name so common had allowed an unscrupulous spammer to make a guess that I was one of the first few thousand addresses to be registered. Clicking 'Unsubscribe' had merely revealed me to be an active recipient.

'Are all spammers so unscrupulous?'

'Is the chief rabbi Jewish?'

Patiently, I was shown how to minimize the invasiveness of this unwanted barrage. On the bar at the top of Outlook Express is the heading 'Tools' (something similar features in other software). In the menu that drops down from it, 'Message rules' offers a facility entitled 'Mail'. Clicking on the 'New' box allows one to list all the scatological words with which one does not want to be assaulted. Into a clinically unshockable box I typed a dreary list of profanities (some of which I would not otherwise have had to write during the whole course of my life). I then ticked appropriate boxes from the 'Conditions' and 'Actions' options to instruct the messages to be destroyed at the server before it even attempts to deliver them to my inbox. I then followed a similar process to ensure that messages from the domain names that are most commonly used for spam are sent straight to 'Deleted items' instead of my inbox. There they wait, out of sight, until I can summon the energy to inspect them and make sure before completely eliminating them that a message from an innocent friend is not inadvertently lost.

These actions have dramatically reduced the amount of spam I have to deal with, although they have not removed it altogether. I will connect to the internet now and call up my e-mails to see what has arrived over the course of a weekend . . .

Well, out of three dozen messages there are five that I wish I had not received. The filter has successfully sent them straight to my 'Deleted items' box, but did not destroy them before they arrived on my screen. According to the subject line, one offers to sell me 'Valium, Prozac or Viagara'. ('Viagra' is one of the words that should have triggered the elimination of the message, but it has been incorrectly spelt.) One tells me 'You've won!' (However, I'm not enough of a loser to want to find out more.) One is trying to interest me in 'On-line gaming'. ('Gaming' will now join 'casino' on my list of banned words.) The title of the next one is 'Peter, it is ages since I heard from you'. (Experience suggests that the use of my Christian name is a strong clue that this is spam inviting me to pay for entry to a porn site, but I haven't added it to the list of profanities because it is quite possible that a friend would use my name in the title of an e-mail. More of a giveaway on this occasion is the fact the sender is named Candy9835kDc85!). The last one is offering me breast enlargement. (And that I could not have anticipated even in the most bizarre moments of the mail-censoring process!)

The statistics suggest that I may even now be getting away lightly. Figures released by the e-mail security firm Message Labs in May 2003 revealed that for the first time more than half of all e-mails sent world-wide were spam (at 55.1% the figure had leapt by one third since the previous month and has risen steadily ever since). The 10 billion spam e-mails that are currently sent every day are expected to rise to 30 billion by the end of 2005. The year in which the bombardment began in earnest was 2002, with a twenty-fold increase between the beginning of the year and its end. In an experiment to research the problem, brand new e-mail accounts were observed in order to investigate how quickly spam would reach them – the fastest was nine minutes.[1]

And yet the apparently vast size of the phenomenon disguises how small its source may be – up to 90 per cent of all junk mails appear to be sent by about 180 'professional' spammers. As far as they are concerned, the compelling attraction of sending unsolicited bulk e-mail is that it costs them virtually nothing. The cost of downloading their advertisement is borne almost entirely by the person who receives it. In this respect it is conspicuously different from telemarketing or junk mail that arrives through the post. The spammer can afford only one recipient in a million to take up the offer or fall for the con. However, if a business is to 'cold call' a potential customer it needs to print leaflets, pay postage, or employ telephonists to work at a call centre. Tiresome though it is to have a romantic dinner for two interrupted by an offer of cut-price double glazing, there is at least modesty and courtesy in the way a telephone sales-person addresses you in your own living room. And a single phone call to the Telephone Preference Service[2] removes the irritation free of charge and for ever by registering your number as one that may not be dialled without consent on pain of a substantial fine. To send a fax to an individual in this way has been made illegal in many countries, including both the UK and the US. But not so spam! And although filtering software such as Spam Assassin or Spam Sieve is becoming sophisticated in being able to tell the difference between 'SEE LEONARDO NUDE' (the fake DiCaprio photos that you can't stomach) and 'See Leonardo's nudes' (the exhibition of da Vinci masterpieces that you can't miss), spammers are constantly finding inventive ways to outwit the sentries.

The term itself is not an acronym, but is one of scores of catchphrases that derive from the classic television comedy series *Monty Python's Flying Circus*. A sketch first broad-cast in 1969 is set in a restaurant where a couple ask the waitress what is available on the menu and are told:

Well, there's egg and bacon; egg sausage and bacon; egg
and spam; egg bacon and spam; egg bacon sausage and
spam; spam bacon sausage and spam; spam egg spam
spam bacon and spam; spam sausage spam spam bacon
spam tomato and spam . . . spam spam spam egg and
spam; spam spam spam spam spam spam baked beans
spam spam spam . . . or lobster thermidor á crevette with
a mornay sauce served in a provencale manner with
shallots and aubergines garnished with truffle paté,
brandy, and with a fried egg on top and spam.[3]

Meanwhile a chorus of Vikings sings surreally: 'Spam
spam spam. Lovely spam! Wonderful spam! Spam spam
spam.' The noise from this becomes increasingly loud until
it drowns out all other conversation.

Internet games players in the late 1980s used their role-
play skills in 'multi-user-dungeons' that allowed them to
invent and explore imaginary underground worlds, chat-
ting to each other in fantasy roles. An antisocial habit
developed of a player responding to a turn of events
of which he did not approve by typing the word 'spam'
repeatedly into the electronic conversation, mimicking
Monty Python's singing vikings, or using one of the computer's automated functions to repeat the word thousands
of times until the programme crashed, ruining everyone's
game. In 1993, with an increase in the popularity of 'newsgroups' (internet conferencing systems that allow people in
far-distant locations to follow threads of conversation
about any subject they choose), the term came to be used
for posting the same message in many, many places.
Although intensely annoying, most such newsgroups have
a code of conduct and are moderated, so it is possible
to remove rants that abuse the spirit of their purpose.
However, it proved much more difficult to prevent pillagers
devising computer programmes to harvest the addresses of

people who post messages in order to create mailing lists for junk mail. That is how the term evolved from playful to infuriating to iniquitous.

The product itself is as innocent as a sandwich! Spam was invented in Texas by George A. Hormel in 1937 to add to his range of economical canned foods. He had wanted to market his pork loaf as ham, but the relevant government department overruled this because it used pork shoulder instead of rump. The name Spam was the winning entry in a competition held during a boozy party at his estate – a slurred elision of shoulder, pork, spice and ham. Hormel Foods have come late and grudgingly to recognize that the colloquial expression is reviving the sales of the product they initially thought it was slandering!

E-mail spam includes every variety of activity that in the days before household computers would be undertaken by people whose activities now sound almost quaint – quacks, hucksters, con men, counterfeiters, cozeners and pimps. James Gleick, a commentator on the impact of the information technology revolution bundles them all together as liars and evildoers: 'The well is poisoned. The social costs are immeasurable: people fear participating in the collective life of the net, and trust is destroyed. [Some call it] the organised crime of the internet.'[4]

Simon James is a computer network administrator whose projects include the London Grid for Learning, which supports the development of information technology in schools. One of his tasks is to protect schoolchildren from accidentally (or deliberately!) stumbling upon pornography during information technology lessons. It is not a task to be taken lightly: 'Every day between ten and one hundred thousand unwanted e-mails are destroyed before they reach the London Borough of Southwark.' It is an expensive business – last year over £6 billion was spent by businesses in Europe alone to tackle the problem. The alternative, however, is a network that begins to slow, e-mails that habitually get lost, and the genuine fear of a crash of the entire global system – the end of the most revolutionary communication system since the telephone.

But Simon sees the responsibility as a shared one: 'Of course spam is not good, and the techniques that are designed to stop it are becoming more and more clever. For example, there is software being developed that can scan a photograph to deduce what percentage of it is skin tone. But it will also analyse the words that go with it so that it can block porn, but allow through a doctor's analysis of a child's eczema.

'But at the end of the day people are stupid if they don't help themselves by taking common sense precautions. For example, never give out details of your bank account in an e-mail. Anyone who asks for it is trying to defraud you. This is completely different from using your credit card to buy books from Amazon or food from Tesco on-line. Reputable companies such as those encrypt the number you type in, putting it into a code which only you and the shop have the key to unlock.

'Don't give your e-mail address out freely. Only send it to people and organizations you feel you can trust. If necessary, set up a separate free account for newsletters or chat rooms so that your personal account remains private. And delete anything that looks suspicious without opening it. If you reply to one, you only have yourself to blame!

'And report anything you object to. Spam Cop is an organization that will track down the system administrator who handled the spammer's bulk e-mail and make a complaint on your behalf.[5] Responsible internet service providers will then take action against people who are abusing their system.'

Organizations that campaign against spam, such as the UK-based Spamhaus Project[6] admit that it is not strictly illegal. It should be, they argue, because it is effectively a theft of service. In May 2002 the European Parliament took its first steps toward agreeing a directive about the processing of personal data and the protection of privacy in the electronic communications sector, and that will guide legislation banning spam throughout the member countries. And in April 2003 the service provider America Online (AOL) filed five federal lawsuits in Virginia, USA, seeking $10 million of damages from unknown defendants (only by starting legal action could they initiate the process of tracking them down). They cited eight million individual complaints from customers.

However, the internet recognizes no national boundaries, and spammers can be light on their feet, moving from country to country with disposable identities in order to find compliant service providers. For as long as e-mails can be sent without an identifier that can be authenticated, ending the problem will be very difficult. There is also a certain amount of resistance from corporations that understandably want to protect their right to use e-mail to advertise by legitimate means to people who have agreed to receive it – 'opt-ins'. (I don't, for instance, want to stop getting information every Thursday from my local cinema complex giving me the times of performances – I'm very happy to be tempted by that kind of movie!) It is widely agreed that it may be some years before anti-spam laws with teeth are ready to bite.

Campaigners have a refreshingly idealistic attitude. The rationale behind the organization Spam Abuse is that bulk unsolicited e-mail is not in the spirit of the internet. Passionate and forceful, its website argues that the internet is one of the few forces that shape the world in which the rules and policy have genuinely been created from the bottom up. It has been self-regulating and self-healing. In that sense it genuinely has created a community that is able to do good. A repressive government can rip down a poster denouncing its actions to a dozen locals in a street, but it cannot stop a website carrying the message to a billion people across the globe.

One such website belongs to Héritiers de la Justice (Inheritors of Justice), a human rights organization in the Democratic Republic of Congo working in partnership with Christian Aid and other development agencies. It has been highlighting abuses of the rights of African people since 1995. In 2000 there was renewed conflict in the region and they published a report highlighting the resultant suffering of the poorest Congolese communities. Publishing this made the organization's position precarious and there were warnings of violence and sinister threats. When the organization was founded it used to take sixteen days to get information about occurrences like this out of the country through unreliable and dangerous means. However, their organization has now been able to access the internet and they were able to publicize their vulnerable position on their website and call for help from the wider world.[7] Pressure from key figures around the globe began to exert its influence not in sixteen days, but in eighteen hours. Within a day the Congolese authorities were inundated with unsolicited e-mails and telephone calls from around the world. With such evident solidarity around the globe for the Héritiers de la Justice cause, the authorities were forced to intervene. Surely this was not spam; it was spirit! However, before the possibilities of the internet rising to become the salvation of the world are overinflated, it is as well to recall that 70 per cent of the world's population has never seen a telephone, let alone a computer.

The biggest threat that spam brings, says Spam Abuse, is that trust breaks down in the internet community:

> Unless we utterly overhaul the internet's mail and news software to charge a mailing fee, spam is taking advantage of the co-operative nature of the net . . . Right now spammers are using unethical tactics, stealing resources from sites and users, to try to get a leg up on people who follow the rules . . . People are much likelier to take net commerce seriously if they don't think of the net as a cesspool of scams, questionable products and pyramid schemes . . . People must not be allowed to become afraid to participate.[8]

Their vision for a community of mutually beneficial solidarity is reminiscent of the church in Jerusalem in the years after Jesus' resurrection, in which 'All the believers were one in heart and mind. No one claimed that any of his possessions was his own, but they shared everything they had.'[9] This makes it slightly dispiriting to discover that one of the first large-scale spams came from a Christian source. On 18 January 1994 the subject line 'Global alert for all: Jesus is coming soon' appeared simultaneously in thousands and thousands of places. Posted by a North American student called Clarence L. Thomas IV, it interpreted current world events as a sign of God withdrawing his Holy Spirit from the earth, and exhorted readers to take the Ten Commandments and the book of Revelation seriously.[10]

It was not the very first. A chain letter headed 'MAKE MONEY FAST' had been appearing in multiple inboxes or newsgroups since the late 1980s. It was an electronic version of a long-standing scam that urged people to give a small amount of money to the sender in the hope of receiving many times that amount from the large number of people to whom they forwarded it. But the damage it could do was limited. The 'Jesus is coming' spam is the one which has become notorious in internet lore. The purists who made up the internet community in those early days debated what they saw as an abuse of the system with outrage. With typical restraint they sum up their response (a torrent of individual furious replies) as, 'He was punished!'

His punishment could have been worse. For the young church in Jerusalem the stakes were higher. As persecution began to threaten, the Christians strengthened their membership by pooling property. Wealthier landowners sold their estates so that the money could contribute toward creating a community with equal access to resources. A man called Joseph is singled out as particularly generous in selling a field and donating the proceeds to be shared out among poorer Christians. Renamed Barnabas ('the encourager') he subsequently had a significant role alongside Paul as one of the first travelling missionaries.

However, a community of ten thousand men and women was bound to contain people who did not share the scrupulous idealism of the leaders. Joseph's generosity is contrasted with a couple called Ananias and Sapphira, who voluntarily sold a property as he did, but kept back part of the money that had been realized for their personal use:

Peter said, 'Ananias, how is it that Satan has so filled your heart that you have lied to the Holy Spirit and have kept for yourself some of the money you received for the land? Didn't it belong to you before it was sold? And after it was sold, wasn't the money at your disposal? What made you think of doing such a thing? You have not lied to men but to God.' When Ananias heard this, he fell down and died. And great fear seized all who heard what had happened.[11]

It is interesting that he and his wife, who suffered the same fate, were denounced not because of a lack of generosity, but because of their dishonesty about the profit they had made. One might have expected them to be applauded at least for making an effort to contribute. Their draconian punishment was not for making money, but for destroying the trust of a community that aspired to perfection. For the first time there was suspicion and fear in a group that had been brought together by their awe of the Holy Spirit.

That too is the strongest criticism that is levelled against spammers. Steve Linford runs the Spamhaus Project as a not-for-profit organization from London headquarters. It protects businesses and companies by filtering their e-mail and is at the forefront of a world-wide campaign for anti-spam laws. He writes: 'The fundamental thing about spammers is that they're all chronic liars. Whatever they tell you is a lie. You opted in to my list – that's a lie. I don't send porn spam – a lie. I'm going to sue you – another lie. They never will.'[12]

It was, perhaps, naive to hope that a community to which access was free, equal and mutually beneficial could thrive as a society of uncomplicated goodness without intervention by those who see the opportunity of profit. And that is true both of the internet and of the first Christian communities. Paul, writing to his protégé Timothy a mere three decades after the resurrection of Jesus, already needed to warn of people who will muscle into Christian leadership because they see the church community as a place where money can be made. He warns the trainee leader not to come under the influence of those who teach 'false doctrines and do not agree to the sound instruction of our Lord Jesus Christ' because although it will prove impossible to stop them they are actually 'men of corrupt mind, who have been robbed of the truth and who think that godliness is a means to financial gain'.[13] The combination of the lie that unsettles people's trust in what is being presented to them and the corruption of a system that relies on integrity in order to bring financial gain is a potent one. It has undermined idealistic societies at every turn of history. In 1587, the Puritan preacher George Gifford wrote his *Discourse of the Subtill Practices of Devilles by Witches and Sorcerers*. His timeless insight was that 'This is man's nature, that where he is persuaded that there is the power to bring prosperity and adversity, there he will worship.'

Reputable Christian organizations such as the Christian E-mail Service take pains on their websites to stress their opposition to spam and their intention that addresses used on their bulletin boards will never be passed on for other purposes. And so they should. As Jesus' followers read the signs of the times, they need to be engaging with the culture in ways that rejoice in its potential for a mission of righteousness, such as the Christians who support Héritiers de la Justice in opposing evil, but deplore attempts to deafen the global electronic ear with pornography, black marketeering, fraud . . . or hectoring proselytism.

Writing to one of those idealistic young Christian communities, Paul wrote: 'Unlike so many, we do not peddle the word of God for profit. On the contrary, in Christ we speak before God with sincerity, like men sent from God.'[14] We would do well to address the idealistic young internet community with the same attitude.

Notes

1 Figures from James Gleick, *What Just Happened?: A Chronicle from the Electronic Frontier*, Abacus, 2002.
2 In the UK, dial 0845 0700707.

3 *Monty Python's Flying Circus: Just the Words*, Methuen, 1998.
4 'Tangled up in spam', *New York Times*, 9 February 2003.
5 http://spamcop.net
6 www.spamhaus.org
7 www.heritiers.org
8 http://spam.abuse.net
9 Acts 4:32.
10 The original e-mail is cached by Google at http://groups. google.com/groups?selm=9401191510AA18576%40jse. stat.ncsu.edu
11 Acts 5:3–5.
12 'Get out of my inbox', *The Observer*, 2 March 2003.
13 1 Timothy 6:3–5.
14 2 Corinthians 2:17.

8

txt

Pls 4give me if U think txt msgs R an outrage. I intnd 2 stop wrtng like this ASAP. But 2 NE1 who has a mobl phn it has bcum 2nd nature.

;-)

The use of txt msgs is chngng the way we spll, rel8 & communic8. It cn only get wrs Bcos it was Xpectd th@ by Jan 04 there wd B 1,467,000,000 mobl phns in the wrld (ie, mor than cnvenshnal phns).

The full name 4 txt is SMS (AKA Shrt Msging Srvice). It was intrdced 2 the UK in 94. 4 a stndrd r8 of 10p a msg of up 2 Xctly 160 chractrs cn B sent. I push of a bttn snds the msg & a x2 bleep tlls the recipient it has arivd. In ordr 2 get the mxmum no of wrds in I msg teens invntd 4 thmslvs a way of shrtnng wrds. It also saves the Fort of typng evry lttr acur8ly, wich is Iborius evn wth predctiv txt, a faclty th8 maks the phn gess wot wrd U R tryng 2 spll. Brvty is also mportnt Bcos teens hav Bgun 2 suffr frm RSI in their thumbs.

Wen U cum 2 trnsl8 a txt, sounds R mor imprtnt thn spllng. Vwls R oftn drppd (eg 'I hv dn my hm wrk', wich is shrt 4 'I hv dn my hm wrk'). Nmbrs take the place of sllbls th@ sound smlar (eg, 'NE1 4 10is?'). Acronyms R used AOTP. Figrs turnd sideways (clld 'emoticons') indic8 the tone of a msg. A cheeky msg cld B shown by a face wiv a tng stckng out thus :-P while 0:-) means 'U R an angl'. This is vtal bcos U can't hear or C the emoshns of a msg like U can in a cnvrsashn or lttr.

A FAQ is wethr txt wll bcum so cmmnplce th@ it wll chng the lnguag. Alrdy sum txt abbrvshns R lstd in the *OED* & the edishn of *Collins* dicshnry pblshed in Jul 03 lstd 'weblish' as their clectiv name.

In Sept 02 a 13-yr-o grl in the W of Scot shckd her tchr by sbmttng an SA on 'My smmr hols' ntirely in txt. There was a gr8 deb8 in the nshnl nwspprs re freedm of Xprsshn v stndrds. Judith Gillespie of the Scot Prnt-Tchr Cncil sd, 'There must be rigorous efforts from all quarters of the education system to stamp out the use of texting as a form of written language so far as English study is concerned.'[1]

½wit!

Mor B9 rplies pointd out th@ Eng Lang is cnstntly chngng & th@ pupls' new ntrst in it cn B Xploitd. Like a diallct (Afro-Carib patois is gvn as a cmprsn) there R times wn it is apprpri8 & times wn RECEIVED PRONUNCIATION AND SPELLING ARE OBLIGATORY. Chn cn B tort the dffrnce. 'It is quick, attractive and uncomplicated,' sd Cynthia McVey, a Glsgw Uni psycho, 'I can understand the frustration of teachers. I think it is important that they get across to their pupils that text messaging is for fun, but that learning to write proper English is vital for their career or future study.'[2]

{ :-\

Wn the 1st txt msg was snt in 92, it was nvr imgnd th@ it wd bcum the most sgnfcnt fetur of the mbl phn. It was offerd as an axesry bcos the tchnlgy was avlble, but in 03 wrtng ovrtook spkng as the bggst use 4 a cllphn. On avrg 2.2 mlln msgs R snt evry hr & the bggst dmnd is @ 00.00 on Nw Yrs Eve. Mar 03 was the mnth that rcordd the bggst use of txt so far, wiv 1.72 blln msgs sent.[3] The no had x2-ed in 12 mnths. The grtst no was snt on Mothrng Sun. Txt is a vry cheap way 2 snd yr ma a rose

. . .

Bt as well as Bng a cheap way 2 communic8, it is also a long-distnc 1 & that is chngng the way we rel8. From a safe dstnc, ppl feel abl 2 say thngs by txt th@ they dare nt say :-) 2 :-). A srvey rveald th@ 42% of usrs aged 15–24 use txt 2 flirt & it has bcum cmmnplce 2 Xchng msgs aftr a d8 as a way of sayng gdnite or sumthng mor ntm8 (IYKWIM).[4] 19% hav usd txt sxsfly 2 ask sum1 on a d8 & 37% hav snt a msg sayng 'I luv U' (4 about ½ it was the 1st time they hd used those wrds). But mor wrryngly 13% hav tld sum1 th8 a relashnshp is ovr thru an SMS msg. It is Ezy 2 tell sum1 U don't wnt 2 C them again if U don't hav 2 C the tears. But th8 wll hav prfnd mplcashns 4 the way a relashn-shp is made, bcos it wll B strtd in the knowlij tht just 2 bleeps cd end it.

It was drng 03 th@ the ptntial 4 txt as a srious mdium bgan 2 B Xplord. It was used 2 snd out 52 mlln GCSE rslts & on 01/05/03 it was used 4 the 1st time as a way 2 vote in lcal Lecshns. Bttr qlty phns wiv mprovmnts in colr & dsply made txt the bst way to get nstnt footy rslts & stck markt news. TV led the way wiv votes 4 ntractv prgrms such as Ch 4's Bg Bro. As a rslt MDA[5] 4casts contud growth. The bggst ncreas is Xpctd 2 B in bsness, Bcos txt is an Fectiv way 4 a co 2 tlk 2 its cnsumrs. Howvr the new tchnlgy MSM[6] wll allow NE1 2 + pix, snds & vids 2 their txt msgs (if they R preprd 2 spnd £££ on new, Xpnsive hnd-sts). There is hstashn in sum ¼s Bcos Xcitemnt in the pst has been prmture (ovr-hypd WAP phones[7] that cnncted 2 the www did not attrct cstmrs as Xpctd) but this time Xpctashns R high th@ ppl will B prprd 2 pay 4 a real rvlushn in the way we communic8. Katrina Bond, of the resrch co Analysys, Xplains: 'After years of growth, pretty much anyone in Britain who wants a mobile has got one . . . The only way to make more money is to get us to see our phones in a new way – as something more than just to make calls.'[8]

Meanwhl Xns hav bn CAPITALISING on the pssblties. The emoticon 4 a Xn is usly +:-) wile teens nvite frnds to chch by txting \o/ (prsmbly Xpcting a srvic of chrsmtic praz). On Gd Fri 02 in Sngapor 150 chchs hired an agncy 2 txt a msg to thsnds of teens: 'Thank me it is Friday. Signed God.' The rslts were :-@. Sum thort it was a joke & LOL. Sum cnfssd their sns. Sum wnt 2 chch ntrigd. The cmpagn 1 an advrtsers' awrd @ the Cannes Fstivl.

In Grmny the Gspl Yoof Chch of Hanover has creatd a vrtual chch using SMS 2 dlver a 5-pt srvic each Sun. It snds a gretng, a bbl redng, a srmon, a prayr & a blssng. They R all 160 chrctrs lng, wiv time 2 rflct btwn each or txt bck a prayr rqest.

The satircl Xn wbsit Ship of Fools hd cvrage in nashnl nwspprs wen it ran a cmptshn 2 rite a txt vrshn of the Lrd's Prayr, reducng it from 372 chrctrs 2 only 160. The wnnng Ntry was by Matthew Campbell, a hstry stdnt from York Uni. His sggeschn was: 'Dad@hvn, UR spshl. We want wot U want & urth 2B like hvn. Giv us food & 4giv sins lyk we 4giv uvaz. Don't test us! Save us! Bcos we no UR boss, UR tuf & UR cool 4eva! OK?'

The shortst Ntry, from Andy Keulemans of Wrexham, was =ly clvr: 'Hi Pa. Matt 6:9–13 again pls. Cheers. CU in chch.'[9]

Simon Jenkins, dvisr of the comp, drew attnshn 2 how appropri8 txt is 4 prayr bcos it spks of the closenss & axesablty of God. He sd: 'Mobile phones are creating an expectation that no one should be further away than a phone call, no question should have to wait for an answer, and no place on earth should be out of contact. Even the wilderness itself will be wired.' But he goes on 2 lment 'an absolute, excessive crowdedness, a loss of personal space every bit as real as that experienced by commuters on a tightly packed train'.[10]

He is ✓ 2 say th@ a txt msg prayr rmnds us th@ God always

lstns, bt it wd B × 2 Ncurij chn 2 eq8 prayng wiv txtng. Txt has givn us the impreshn th@ evry time we ask a queshn it will B anserd instntly. But our sprtul relashnshps R v v difrnt. The mtafors we use 2 dscrib our relijus lives R a srch, a jrny, a wlk. They spk of lng periods of time nvestd (sumtims Nlightnng; sumtims wastd) & deep Xtendd thort. Wen Shkspr's Hamlet askd, '2 B / not 2 B = ?' he did nt Xpect an ansr 2day or 2moro. How cn we Ncurij NE yng :-)-^< or :-)8-< th@ Ckng the luv of God is worth persvrng wiv 4 yrs, wen a msg of luv 2 a grlfrnd or boyfrnd gets a rply in 10 secs SWALK? Our hope mst B th@ as the mkng & brkng of relashnshps speeds, ppl wll look 1ce agn 2 God 4 the fathflnss they can't find in NE uva way. As the OT says of God: Tho the /_/_/\ B shkn & the ^-^-^ B remvd yet my luv 4 U wll nt cum 2 an .[11]

As life grows fstr, we R fndng it Esier 2 adapt 2 sum thngs thn uvaz. We hav gobld up the cnvnyuns meal th@ cooks in secs wivout hvng 2 chp a sngl vgtbl. We 1der how we mangd B4 we cd wthdrw £££ from a bnk 24/7. Wot nxt? Praps the microwv heatr th@ wll giv us a lng, rlaxng pm in frnt of the fire in 8 mins! If we cum 2 Xpect th@ a microwv prayr durng the comershul brk of a TV prog wll B enuf 2 sustn the totly fulfld life th@ JC prmisd we cn only B disapointd. The NT tlls us: 'JC is the same ystrday & 2day & 4eva.'[12] A chngng O needs an unchngng God.

Wiv txt WUCIWUG. But 'O the dpth of the rchs of the wsdm & knolij of God!' as the NT tlls us.[13] In JC the wrd Bcame flsh. Hvn hlp us if the flsh Bcums txt!

THNQ 4 pttng up wiv this.

Cya.

PG

Notes

1 Quoted in the *Sunday Herald*, 2 March 2003.
2 Dr Cynthia McVey, lecturer in psychology at Glasgow Caledonian University, ibid.
3 *What Cellphone?*, May 2003.
4 MORI research for Lycos UK, September 2000.
5 Mobile Data Association.
6 Multimedia Messaging Services.
7 Wireless Application Protocol.
8 *The Observer*, 22 September 2002.
9 www.ship-of-fools.com
10 *Third Way*, June 1999.
11 Isaiah 54:10.
12 Hebrews 13:8.
13 Romans 11:33.

9

Businesses that Change Their Name

I have just put down the telephone after a conversation with my father. I am slightly unsettled. We had been having a rather boring conversation about how to stop people accidentally sending us each others' mail when he announced, 'Of course, you know that your great-grandfather changed our surname, don't you?' Indeed I did not! 'He was born Robert Grayston, but for reasons that he took with him to the grave he decided to add an E to the end.' A little bit of research has confirmed this as true. He was born a Grayston in Ipswich in 1854, but he died a Graystone in North London in 1917. In between he earned a trade as a boot maker, and among his clients was Tottenham Hotspur Football Club.

For forty-four years I have been carrying around an E that does not belong to me. It has been weighing heavily on my shoulders all day.

As an individual, it is not difficult at all to change your name. In fact in UK law anyone over sixteen can choose what they want to be called and establish it simply by using the name regularly. To make it official and require others to use your new name necessitates a deed poll – one of the simplest of all legal documents, signed by a single witness and carried around so that it can be produced whenever it is called for. There are no restrictions whatever on what you can be known as – even inserting 'Baroness' or 'Sir' in front of the name your parents gave you is legal provided you are not doing so for a fraudulent purpose. You need to be eighteen (or to have parental consent) in order to sign a deed poll. If you change your name to your husband's on your wedding day the marriage certificate acts as a deed poll as well. The same is true if you change it to your wife's, which is completely acceptable although not traditional, but opting for a double-barrelled name requires the legal document.

Although changing your name is a personally significant and sometimes emotional experience, the stakes are not nearly so high as when a business changes its name. Since the turn of the century it has happened with such increasing regularity that a small but lucrative industry has built up around it, with consultancies such as Name Lab and Interbrand being established in order to maximize the potential of the name under which a business trades.

In years past a change of name was an admission that something was deeply wrong with a business or product; recently changing your name is more likely to be a recognition that something could be better. A subtle sign of the times!

If you are able to, cast your mind back one generation. In 1957 there was a serious fire at the site of a nuclear reactor in Cumbria and massive clouds of radioactive energy were released. The incident generated a panicky national debate about the safety of nuclear power, during which the name Windscale became associated with all our unspoken anxieties about the human race's ability to bring about its own destruction. Although the site has never been officially renamed, its operators insisted that in all publicity it should be referred to by the name of the town in which it is situated – Sellafield. However, changing its name did not generate large-scale goodwill on the part of a suspicious public. The change of name was not matched by such significant organizational changes as to regenerate confidence.

The lessons about how rapidly fortunes can change are even more bruising when the name of the company is also the name of an individual. In the 1980s the jewellery retail chain Ratners, which specialized in selling pretty items of modest quality to a mass market, was a spectacular success on the high street. Its founder and chairman, Gerald Ratner, was a popular after-dinner speaker who endeared himself to his fellow businessmen with his self-deprecating humour. In 1991 he made the mistake of using his usual knockabout style in front of an audience of journalists. He described the astonishment with which his rivals in the jewellery trade looked at his profit margins on products such as a silver-plated tray and goblets, which were on sale for a remarkably low price: '"How do you manage to sell a product like that so cheap?" they ask me. And I am happy to tell them the secret: "Because it is total crap"!' He went to bed content that the gales of laughter which followed had maintained his popularity, but woke up to find that the last two words of his joke were a headline in the *Sun* newspaper. The tabloid-buying public, who formed the core of his customers, was humiliated to discover that the chairman had such a low opinion of his stock – and by implication of the people who purchased it. Consumer confidence was torpedoed, the shops emptied, and the company was brought to the brink of bankruptcy. For a short while 'ratner' became a slang term for anything one would step aside to avoid on the pavement. The firm responded quickly by demanding the resignation of its own founder and renaming itself Signet. It directed attention toward the other brands owned by the parent company, particularly H. Samuel and Ernest Jones, both of which present themselves to the public as trusted places where high-class products can be sought out. Experts suggest that it takes ten to fifteen years for a major gaffe to be forgiven, and in Signet's case it took until the end of the decade for a strong trading statement to be re-established – their sales leading up to the turn of the century were a record. A signet ring is not only a piece of jewellery but a seal that authenticates a document and reveals its true value – perfectly summing up the image the company wanted the public to associate with its products.

Some firms in the arrogant economic climate of the 1980s felt that they could brazen out bad publicity. It seemed that sea otters had been hunted to extinction for their pelts until a tiny colony was found in Alaska and helped, cub by cub, back into a substantial population. Then on Good Friday 1989 the supertanker Exxon Valdez spilled ten million gallons of oil into the sea in the Prince William Sound and killed twelve thousand at a stroke. It devastated 25,000 square kilometres of the coast's ecosystem. Reckoning up the enormous cost of delivering a new identity to go with a new name, Exxon decided to make no change. The catastrophe had virtually no impact on its share price. They did, however, change the name of the ship itself. It can still be glimpsed sailing off the coast of Scotland but its present name, Sea River Mediterranean, suggests a very different and altogether sunnier history.

Recent years have, however, seen an escalation in the frequency with which names of both products and businesses have been changed – and in some cases changed back again. The motives have been varied, but far from being a nervous reaction to bad news they have almost all been characterized by an expensive and thoroughly researched planning process. The increasing globalization of the market for goods at the end of the last century was one of the causes, because it brought with it a need for 'world brand unity'. Most memorable, perhaps because being among the first it took the people by surprise, was the renaming of Marathon, the chocolate bar stuffed with nougat and peanuts, as Snickers. This brought the UK name in line with the North American one (it has always been considered that the US market is more resistant to change). The same reason is given for the refined and gemlike sweets Opal Fruits becoming the pyrotechnic Starburst. The moisturizing cream Oil of Ulay was rebranded as Oil of Olay to standardize its name across Europe, and the household cleaner Jif became Cif rather than the other way round because of the difficulty of pronouncing the letter J in some European languages.

Other changes took place because the turn of the millennium led to many businesses and organizations examining their public image and associating the desire to provide services that genuinely meet contemporary requirements with the need for a name that implies freshness and energy. Hence Amicus, Altria, Accenture, Elementis, HSBC, Aviva, Going Places, Uniq and Corus. If you would like to approach this as a quiz, don't let your eye stray toward the end of the chapter until you have worked out what you knew them as ten years ago![1]

Tony Thorne, who is the head of the Language Centre at King's College London, has observed the trends closely:

I am very cynical. I hate most of the company names that I hear, either because they are pretentious or phoney, or because they are too timid. Some are too boring – things like 'Logical Network Solutions'. There are millions of companies called things like that, which doesn't inspire one. But I particularly dislike this rash of fake Latinate names that has been so trendy . . . Being a linguist I don't react like a normal person, I suppose, but I think that a lot of normal customers react negatively to these names because they think they are somehow patronising.[2]

It was in 1961 that the naming of companies first began to emerge as a challenge. In that year the number of trade names registered overtook the number of words in the English language. All the good names had been taken! So for five decades there has been an increasing shortage of genuine English words that can be registered as a trademark. The trend in the 1970s was for names that were virtually meaningless, but conjured up images of size and anonymity such as 'General Profitable' or 'Consolidated Incorporated'.

In the next decade retail businesses that had been in the hands of the same family since Victorian times trimmed their names as part of their modernization. The stationer W. H. Smith and Son, which had been renamed once in 1846 after the birth of William Henry Smith the second, dropped 'and Son' to revert to its original name (the directors having toyed with the possibility of the straightforward 'Smiths', by which the majority of its customers knew it anyway). Even Christian organizations saw that subtle changes could allow them to present themselves to the public in a way more fitting to contemporary mores – The Church Missionary Society, eager to rid itself of the negative, colonial associations of the word 'missionary' renamed itself the Church Mission Society.

Elsewhere in Europe the impact of the names of retail outlets was less marked. In Russia, for instance, shops without the pressure of competition had names like 'Bread' or 'Clothes'. The arrival of capitalism in the 1990s saw the expansion of English-speaking companies into the new East European markets, and the need for shoppers to negotiate trade names that were not only difficult to pronounce but also gave no hint of the product for sale.

This accounts in part for the rise in pseudo-Latin names – Potenta, Vividon, Axelerato, Prosperant (all of them invented – it isn't difficult)! They are easy to pronounce in most European languages. In the UK it makes sense for a firm to change its name from one with an Anglo-Saxon root to one that registers meaning across a greater number of languages, which is why there were over 250 name changes last year – a sign of the times for which there is no equivalent in any other part of Europe. Latin syllables also carry a portentousness with them that Anglo-Saxon cannot match. There has been a long-running campaign in the Lincolnshire town of Sibsey by householders in Goosemuck Lane (voted the worst street name in the country) to have their road renamed Littlemoor Close. Historically the road got its name because it was on the farmers' route to Nottingham's goose fair. The words 'goose' and 'muck' both arrived with the Vikings alongside our most enduring swearwords.

The process, as described by the brand strategy consultancy Name Lab,[3] involves a brainstorming interview with the staff of a company to establish positive messages that they want to convey about their products. These are compared with a list of morphemes (the units that make up compound words such as 'pro', which always implies forward, and 'bene', which comes at the start of many words suggesting goodness). Overused syllables are discarded and then the matching morphemes are combined by computer to create every possible variation. Potential names are shortlisted, and their spelling is tinkered with to make them more readily visible as typeset words or easier to pronounce. The names are ordered along a continuum of values (for instance, a business marketing hair shampoo might be called Soothe, Rouse or Zing!), and the possibilities presented to the board of the company. It is, apparently, usual to present 'frightening' choices as well as ones with genuine potential because the emotional and political implications of a change of name are so substantial that a committee never chooses the most interesting or challenging option. It is then easier to find agreement because the board is collectively relieved that it has not opted for the most outrageous of the choices. By law, an extra general meeting must be called because it is the shareholders of a company who hold responsibility for its name. In many cases – for example, the newly renamed hotel and restaurant business Six Continents – only one name is put before shareholders in a straight-forward 'yes or no' vote.

The renaming of Bass as Six Continents has been one of the more successful changes of recent years. It was forced on a company that was reluctant to lose two centuries of historical recognition for 'a pint of Bass' because they sold the brewing business with which the name was associated. Analysts put down its success to the fact that it conveys an immediate meaning, and that it contracts to an appeal-ing nickname – 6C. It was actually the winner from ten thousand entries in a competition among employees. An agency was only used in the final stage, in which interna-tional dictionaries are trawled to check that unforeseen double-meanings in far-flung countries are not allowed to draw the wrong kind of attention to a product or firm.

Past mistakes of this kind are the stuff of legend and, for some reason, the automobile industry is particularly prone. The Rolls Royce Silver Mist was not a success in Northern Europe because in some Scandinavian languages 'mist' is the slang equivalent of 'ratner'. The Chevy Nova faltered in the Latin American countries where 'no va' means 'won't go'. And who could be proud of driving a Pinto in the parts of Mexico where it is a Spanish dialect word for 'little penis'?

A mistake of this kind when naming a product seems endearing; an unsuccessful change of name for a company can be a catastrophe. The consulting arm of PricewaterhouseCooper went, for such a brief moment that you may have missed it, under the name of Monday. Laboriously researched and liberally funded, their rebrand was the result of focus groups in the United States associating the word Monday with enthusiasm, sleeves rolled up to do the best possible job, early morning coffee and doughnuts, and other industrious images. The company was shocked by reactions to the name in Europe, where Monday is the day that flies in like a brick after the weekend. The derision with which some changes of name were coming to be held was summed up by the satirical web magazine B3TA, which dramatically undermined the multi-million dollar renaming exercise that had been focused on a new website. British surfers who used a search engine to investigate the rebrand found themselves reading: 'PricewaterhouseCooper Consulting are changing their name to Monday . . . They have created IntroducingMonday.com . . . Shame they forgot to register IntroducingMonday.co.uk.' Then, as guffawing donkeys danced in the background: 'We've got your name . . . la la la . . . everybody knows!' The rebrand was quietly downsized and Monday swallowed up in IBM Global services. While the original website is now inaccessible on the internet, its parasitical cousin is still there to revel in.[4]

The decision of Philip Morris to change its name to Altria (in Latin, 'altus' means high) has been equally open to scorn. Although the parent group has subdivisions such as Kraft Foods and Miller Brewing, the company's name is most closely associated with cigarettes. The satirical website Satire Wire lost no time in irritating the company in its usual inventive manner:

Just days after Philip Morris declared it will change its

name to the Altria Group, lung cancer today announced that it will change its name to Philip Morris. According to lung cancer officials, the chance to snap up a brand that is more widely associated with lung cancer than lung cancer itself was too enticing to pass up. 'The "lung cancer" brand certainly evokes something powerful and terrible, but that brand essence is palpable only in English-speaking markets,' explained director Reginald Hacking-Coughlin. 'In terms of global markets, it lacks universality. If you're in Spain, you cannot just say lung cancer, you have to say *cáncer de pulmón*. In Germany, it is *lungenkrebs*. "Philip Morris", by contrast, ensures instant, world-wide comprehension. It needs no translation. When you hear Philip Morris you think of lung cancer, no matter whether you speak English or German or Cantonese.'[5]

In the UK the most widely discussed name change of recent years became regarded as a personal affront because it had an impact on something almost everyone does on a daily basis – receiving a letter. In March 2001, following an annual loss of £1.1 billion and 32,000 job losses (representing 16 per cent of the staff) the British Post Office changed its corporate name to Consignia. Jerry Cope, one of the directors, explained the decision: 'The new name describes the full scope of what The Post Office does in a way that the words "post" and "office" cannot. "To consign" means "to entrust to the care of", which is what each of our customers does every day, no matter which of our services they choose.'[6]

The decision to change, with its associated hopes of a change of fortune, failed to take into account the affection that the public had for an institution they treasured. Staff who delivered the post, already demoralized by the redundancy of their colleagues, despaired. It was they who had to meet, beside the letter box, customers who wanted a better service, not a better name. Public relations officers who protested that long-established brand names such as Royal Mail and Parcelforce had not gone away and were still a part of the parent company confused what they intended to clarify. And the discovery that the change had cost £500,000 (not including the more practical expense of changing stationery and signs) but would not stop the cost of posting a letter from rising, aggravated consumers further. Fifteen months later the company acknowledged its mistake and changed its name again – to Royal Mail plc (actually adopting the name of its most popular service, but perceived as a direct reversal of the former change).

All this goes to show that, for good or ill, great power resides in giving something a name. This is also one of the oldest and most enduring religious beliefs. In the ancient pagan world knowing a god's name was supposed to confer control over it, the act of naming something being the right of a superior power. Seven centuries before Jesus, the ancient Greek poet Hesiod wrote his *Theogeny* on the pretext that studying the names of the gods was the route to understanding the circumstances in which to elicit their blessing. But it is even more significant in the Bible that the giving of a name, and more especially the changing of a name, can assert a claim on a person's life that has a profound impact on his or her destiny.

Naming is shown from the beginning to be an action and a prerogative of God. In the myths that occupy the first chapters of the Bible it pleases God to give names to the day and the night, the sea and the sky, and he subsequently asserts his authority over the zenith of his creation by naming it 'humankind'.[7] But he entrusts the work of naming living things to the human mind, 'and whatever the man called each living creature, that was its name'.[8] In this godlike task the man shows godly qualities. In particular, when it comes to naming his partner he chooses a name that sounds the coequal in every breathy detail of his own (the English equivalents 'man' and 'woman' do not do justice to the equality and sexiness of the original Hebrew). However, when sin enters the world the very first way it expresses itself is through a change of name. The man, feeling that the name he originally gave his partner no longer expresses his attitude toward her, inflicts on her the new name Eve. Its Hebrew meaning is 'living'. A name that describes what he appreciates about her is changed perforce to a name that speaks of what he expects from her, 'because she would become the mother of all the living'.[9] The world's first great wickedness involved changing a name in order to dominate. And it was man-made.

As the Bible progresses the giving of names becomes invariably an authority function (surprisingly, in view of the outcome of the name-giving in Eden, a baby's name is given by the mother twenty-eight times and by the father eighteen). A conquering emperor who puts a puppet king in place to protect his interests in the new territories may change his vassal's name in order to make it clear who is boss, which is how King Eliakim comes to wake up one morning and discover he has become King Jehoiakim (both meaning 'established by God' in subtly different ways).[10]

However, when God is the authority who changes a name it sets someone free from the circumstances in which they were born and expresses the potential for a lifetime of fulfilment that has opened for them. Thus it is that the unhappily childless Abram (whose name 'exalted father' must have taunted him as a cruel irony) is renamed Abraham (the implication of which is 'ancestor of a multitude', his true destiny).[11] The younger of the twins born to

Isaac and Rebekah emerges from the womb with his hand on his brother's heel. They name him Jacob which, give or take a play on words, means 'he grabs all he can get'. This name either reflects or shapes the events of his life until a dramatic and violent encounter with God changes his values in every way. The new name Israel, given to him by God, hints at the experience of the entire nation that regards him as its patriarch – it means 'the one that grapples with God'.[12]

When Jesus changed the name of his friend Simon to Peter it was part of the unbroken tradition stretching from the earliest days to contemporary branding that uses the evocative power of a name to give people confidence. Simon derives from the Hebrew word for 'listening', but the Greek name Peter means 'the rock'. Given the poverty of Peter's first attempts to be true to the Christ, it displayed a visionary trust by Jesus in the way potential can triumph over initial inadequacy. While present-day impatience tends to consign inappropriate names to speedy failure, Jesus was clear-sighted in his understanding that a Church which was going to have a global impact needed a leader whose name suggested values in which people could have confidence. 'On this rock I will build my church,' he said of Peter, and in the goodness of God we rejoice to this day that 'the gates of Hades will not overcome it.'[13]

The other great shaper of the Christian Church also underwent a startling rebrand, but with a change of name that would be unlikely to win approval from a corporation's shareholders in this century. Saul of Tarsus, the notorious persecutor of the emerging Christian Church, encountered Jesus in a manner so compelling that he became the Church's first international missionary. As part of his need to put his past behind him and become a credible witness to the world beyond Judaism he changed his Jewish name Saul to its nearest Roman equivalent, Paul.[14] The meaning of Saul is 'an answer to prayer'; the meaning of Paul is 'small and unassuming'. Opting for a Latin name, so favoured by branding consultancies, had the very opposite impact from that which is sought by present day companies – it emphasized humility.

Peter and Paul: the rock and the humble one. So appropriate of the one who changed their lives! I find myself quietly encouraged that the Church, many centuries after Peter and Paul first rejoiced to worship Jesus Christ as their God, still struggles with varying amounts of success to present Jesus to the world both as a rock in whom we can put our trust and a servant whose humble love is genuinely transforming. Not changing names but changing lives! In an age in which organizations repeatedly change their name, I hope and expect that the Christian faith never will.

Notes

1 These were formerly the Amalgamated Electrical and Engineering Union (too many syllables), Philip Morris (too associated with tobacco – the very name sounds like someone coughing), Anderson's Management Consultancy (too tainted by the association of its auditing arm with the allegations of fraud in the Enron corporation), Harrison and Crossfield (too pompous), Midland Bank (too provincial), CGNU – the result of successive mergers between insurance companies Commercial Union, General Accident and Norwich Union (too boring to explain), Pickfords Travel (too antiquated), Unigate (too rustic), and British Steel (what British steel?).

2 *Shop Talk*, BBC Radio 4, 22 October 2002.

3 www.namelab.com

4 www.introducingmonday.co.uk

5 www.satirewire.com

6 Press release, 26 March 2001.

7 Genesis 5:2.
8 Genesis 2:19.
9 Genesis 3:20.
10 2 Kings 23:34.
11 Genesis 17:5.
12 Genesis 32:28.
13 Matthew 16:18.
14 Acts 13:9.

The Naked Chef

Excuse the tears! I have never cooked with real chillies before. Chopping them was irritating my contact lens in a really frustrating way. I didn't deliberately rub my eyes; it was instinctive. Now the sting is excruciating, I can't hold the knife, and I can't read the recipe. On the bright side, though, my contact lens is not bothering me any more.

I feel he ought to have warned me. His recipes are designed with people like me precisely in mind. Everything about the chummy, cheery, take-it-easy nature of his writing style is designed to reassure me that a life full of loyal friendship can be fostered around a lovingly prepared table. As I read the recipe I can hear him telling me precisely what to do (which is not surprising since he chats into a dictaphone and someone else types his words):

> The one thing all these [comfort grub] recipes have in common is memories of childhood; enjoying company round the dinner table, or in my case, coming home shivering and wet from playing footie with the boys and being ordered to change out of my wet clothes into my dressing-gown before being given a steaming bowl of chilli with a jacket potato and a lob of guacamole and yoghurt. Remember: don't eat to live, but live to eat.[1]

And as if to prove it, opposite the recipe is his photograph.

He is walking across a zebra crossing in the pouring rain, caught unexpectedly in a shower on his way home from the local park, water dripping from his tousled hair on to his cherub cheeks. No wonder I want to cook this recipe! How could anyone not want to! He's got me wrapped around his finger – the roguish, charming, talented, naughty little millionaire!

He is, of course, Jamie Oliver. His television series *The Naked Chef* and the books based on it have made his face one of the most recognizable in the UK. Before reaching the age of thirty he rode a rollercoaster track from popularity as television's most likeable celebrity chef, through a damning critical hostility, to being revered as a national treasure.

The title *The Naked Chef* (apart from being a saucy enticement to watch the sole television chef we could conceive of seeing nude without stampeding toward the off switch) refers to the straightforward style of his cookery:

> Using the bare essentials of your larder and stripping down restaurant methods to the reality of home . . . This book isn't about cheffy food, it is for normal people who want shortcuts and tips; people who want to make simple, day-to-day meals different and absolutely fantastic . . . cooking tasty, gutsy, simple, common-sense food and having a right good laugh at the same time.[2]

However, alongside his deliciously appealing way with food, Jamie Oliver offers us a complete and deliciously appealing lifestyle. During the course of the series we have seen him cook for and eat with his wife Juliette Norton ('my missus – sorry – the lovely Jules'), his best man Ben, his best mate Gennaro, and 'all the other nutters I grew up with'. We have seen him gurgle with enthusiasm for good food, slide down the bannisters to the door, leap on his motor scooter to zoom to Borough market (in South London) to buy fresh ingredients, and return from Sainsbury's weighed down with carrier bags as part of a slice-of-life advertising campaign. It is an enviable world – one in which there is hard work, but it is amply rewarded. Friendship (enriched by shared meals) roots a speed-of-light lifestyle in security; loyalty is the best context for family (he and Jules have been together since their teens); love and generosity are given and received; food is far too good for drugs to add anything to life; and meals create a space in which there is room for the features that give existence its true worth. And all this takes place with Jamie's unique commentary, combining working-class slang ('sorted') with a revival of upper-class colloquialisms ('malarkey') in an Essex accent made endearing by a slight speech impediment:

> Baby chard, little bit of rocket, scatter . . . really, really casually . . . yeah, dead tempting to buy those bags of salad . . . pukka peaches (I like the skin, personally) . . . a ripped peach looks so much better than a cut one. Buffalo mozzarella, soft and milky, better than the cheap stuff – rip it into nice little mouth-sized pieces.[3]

Jamie Oliver grew up in the pub his parents owned in Saffron Walden, Essex, and helped out in the kitchen from a early age. He was 'not the brightest banana of the bunch', but mediocre academic results were replaced by high marks when he went to Westminster Catering College in London. He went on to work with some of the country's top chefs, including Antonio Carluccio at his Neal Street restaurant and Rose Gray and Ruth Rogers at the River Café. It was there that he made his first television appearance by accident. In 1997, covering for a colleague who was off sick, he was filmed as part of a BBC documentary that went behind the scenes at the restaurant. Young, talented, and completely natural in front of the camera, he immediately attracted attention. The day after the broadcast he was telephoned by five different production companies. He chose to work with Pat Llewellyn of Optomen, a company with a track record of successful television programmes about food. They made three series together, using a format in which the camera follows his hands and face as he prepares food and she chats to him off-screen. The location was chosen to give the impression that he was cooking and entertaining in his own home.

The programmes were an immediate success. 'I really am quite weak', wrote the television critic Kathryn Flett. 'Just as one should never shop when hungry, so one should never watch Jamie Oliver tearing fruit and pinching fish.'[4] They were quickly followed by the books, the stage show, the video, the crockery collection and the CD (a compilation of the music Jamie listens to while cooking). Subsequently there came many, many appearances in television adverts for Sainsbury's – a campaign that has coincided with a £1 billion increase in the supermarket chain's turnover.

But with ubiquity came a press backlash. The journalist Mark Lawson suggested that Jamie was 'widely derided by pundits as a mockney gobshite whose adverts . . . were as thin and tacky as a supermarket plastic bag'.[5] His colleague Jonathan Freedland went further: 'Jamie Oliver is – like the Lord himself – all around us . . . It is getting hard to spend a single day without seeing his face or hearing his voice. The traditional British reaction to this extreme level of success is resentment and envy – particularly when the star in question is [so young].'[6]

It is difficult to understand the ferocity of the attack. There was no scandal to expose and the quality of the programmes was, if anything, increasing. The principal accusation was that anyone so successful could not be genuine – that the enthusiasm or the accent or the lifestyle must be a hypocritical performance invented in order to amass a fortune.

However, this was about to change radically. Jamie Oliver announced that he planned to open a unique restaurant. Set in an unprepossessing area of London, it was to be a not-for-profit venture that gave fifteen unemployed young people who had not thrived in the state education system an opportunity to train as chefs and gain experience in their first stable jobs. He sank a reckless amount of his own money in the charitable project and sold the right to film it to Channel 4, who changed its name from *Oliver's Army* to *Jamie's Kitchen* and unexpectedly found themselves broadcasting the outstanding documentary series of 2002.

The feature that made the series so compelling was the young people's refusal to follow the conventions that usually characterize the 'script' of heart-warming failure-to-success films. They reacted in mixed ways to the opportunities that were being offered to them. Some skipped college, refused to be grateful, rejected 'last chances' and, when challenged, accused Jamie Oliver of using them to further his own fame and success. Bewildered that they were not all prepared to work with him on this once-in-a-lifetime offer of redemption, his response veered between angry disciplinarian, cajoling teacher and sympathetic mate. When they did not turn up, he sent taxis to their homes. When they refused to make an effort, he pleaded. When they questioned his integrity, he confessed that he remortgaged his home in order to give them this opportunity. He scolded and coaxed, he joked and swore, he confessed to camera that he felt trapped in a nightmare. Jamie's naivety, determination and despair made accusations of insincerity impossible. Of the original fifteen, ten students made it through to the opening night of the restaurant. It was and continues to be a triumph, whose food and service is almost universally lauded. It is still named Fifteen despite the five who walked (or were, after painful soul-searching, sent) away. The experiment is to be repeated in subsequent years and in other countries. Possessing all the qualities needed for success in modern Britain – notably an egalitarian integrity and a social conscience – Jamie Oliver became a media saint. In June 2003 he was awarded an OBE.

When I visited Fifteen, I took my friend Paul Waddell with me. Young, jobless and estranged from his family, life has dealt him many of the disadvantages that the trainee chefs have suffered. We talked animatedly about food for the entire length of the Northern Line. Searching our memories to remember our best ever meals, we agreed that it had been the match of the quality of the company and the excellence of the food that made such occasions outstanding. Mine involved home-made soup around a blazing fire in an ancient pub in Malmesbury, Wiltshire, after walking through freezing fog from morning service in the abbey. His involved chilli con carne around a Playstation late at night in the house of a friend whose parents had gone away for the weekend.

The look of the restaurant is fantastic. It is a relaxed and welcoming room with pink and grey leather banquettes. On the walls are huge, pink mock-graffiti. There is a buzz of warm conversation and immediately attentive staff. I ask for a table for two. A look of disappointment spreads across the waitress's face and she explains that the next available table for two will be in three months. THREE MONTHS! Paul and I exchange disbelieving glances as she checks in vain whether there might be a last-minute cancellation. The scallop crudo with Japanese yuzu lime and pomegranates is carried past, but it is not for me. The fillet of McDuff beef poached in Barbarossa Merlot is on its way to some lucky diner, but it won't be Paul.

And then, as often before, Paul has an idea so inspired that his future success is surely assured despite every setback: 'Blow the McDuff; let's find the McDonald's!' In fact the nearest McDonald's is less than three minutes' walk. Its logo, a yellow M ('the golden arches'), is visible from a great distance and, having recently been confirmed as the most widely recognized brand on the planet, is unmistakeable. 'I used to work at McDonald's,' says Paul. 'I'll tell you all about it. It is a much more interesting sign of the times than *The Naked Chef*!'

It is indeed an interesting comparison since the fifteen young people who were offered an unexpected break in *Jamie's Kitchen* come from a similar background to many of McDonald's' 1.5 million employees in 118 countries. Paul continues, 'I was sixteen and desperate for a job. My mate said, "Let's both apply and work there together; it will be a laugh!" But he didn't turn up for the interview; I did. I had the job within ten minutes. I was working the tills and serving the public within twenty. I was bored out of my skull before lunch.' But surely you had training? 'Training for what? The tills are designed to tell you precisely what to do as you press one button after another. The chips arrive at the restaurant frozen. They are put in a frier at a pre-set temperature and a push-button timer bleeps at precisely the right moment to take them out. Even the salads come already chopped. How much training do you need to assemble a burger in a bun?'

A cheerful young man behind the counter laughs with me as I fumble over ordering the food. Paul wants a Double Quarterpounder meal and Chicken McNuggets. Having heard that McDonald's is responding to a call for healthier food, I ask for a low-fat Chicken Salsa Flatbread. It comes with french fries. They sit on two trays, each item wrapped in its own individual box. I hand over about one twelfth of the money that I would have spent in Fifteen. 'That's why I eat here even though I couldn't stand working here again. It is as cheap as eating at home. You can drive here, eat and leave in less time than it takes to fry an egg in your own kitchen. And you don't wash up; you just throw it all away. The food tastes fine, although it is a bit bland compared with other places. (Have you tried KFC? Gorgeous!) But at least you know exactly what you're going to get, so you are never disappointed.'

He has, unwittingly, identified all four of the 'alluring characteristics' that the American thinker George Ritzer believes to be behind the McDonald's phenomenon: efficiency, calculability, predictability and control.[7] Efficiency involves employees working in a strictly regulated way that maximizes their output, and customers finding the surest way to progress from being hungry to being full. Calculability creates a context in which objective quantity seems more significant than subjective quality. Size and time matter – a *Big* Mac comes with *large* fries in *less than* one minute. Predictability ensures that Chicken McNuggets taste the same whether they are eaten in Birmingham, Alabama, or Birmingham, England (requiring ingenuity with artificial flavourings since the beef tallow in which they were fried in the USA is not used in the UK in deference to the large Hindu population). Every single McDonald's french fry is from a Russet Burbank potato cut to 7 mm thick. Control is most noticeable in the attempt to substitute any skill that might be required of an employee with an automated system, meaning that labour is cheap and easily replaceable. 'We cannot trust some people who are non-conformists,' said one of the founders. 'The organization cannot trust the individual; the individual must trust the organization.'[8] However, in more subtle ways the customers too are controlled – with queues to be served, limited menus, and hard seats encouraging them to eat quickly, leave and return.

Which they do in their millions! In the UK 2.5 million people eat at a McDonald's every single day. One in every two hundred of the world's population will eat in one of their stores today. There are more than 30,000 restaurants world-wide, and it is highly likely that four new ones will have opened by the time you wake up tomorrow morning. The values and tastes of America have become, in many respects, the homogenized culture of the entire McWorld. This is as true in Kuwait (where in 1994 the queue of cars at the drive-in on its opening day stretched for seven miles) as it is in Zimbabwe (where an Australian documentary *Hamburgers in Harare* featured an African man who said, 'I don't want to eat local foods any more . . . This is my culture now. It is inside me.')[9]

Richard and Maurice ('Mac') McDonald opened their first restaurant in Pasadena in 1937. It cashed in on California's new craze for drive-in restaurants. As in all the others, customers drove into the car park where orders were taken and food brought to the vehicle by attractively dressed young waitresses – 'carhops'. It was modestly successful. But it was in 1948 at a new building in San Bernadino that they made their world-changing innovation by applying the principles of a factory assembly line to their kitchen. They reorganized it so that one worker grilled the meat, another put it inside the bread and added relish, a third wrapped it, while others took the orders. At the same time they deleted from their menu anything that required a knife or fork in order to eat it, and replaced their crockery with disposable paper plates and cups. At a stroke their

'Speedee Service System' had reduced the need for training, washing-up and waiters. They employed fresh-faced young men instead of teenage girls, making the restaurant attractive to families instead of the adolescent boys who had previously honked their horns, scared the neighbours and nicked the cutlery. It allowed them to reduce the price of their hamburgers from 35 cents to 15 cents. In response to a phenomenal success they designed a new building, custom-made to increase speed and raise the volume of sales. On both sides of its sloping roof were arches forming the letter M, picked out at night in yellow neon.

It was a man named Ray Kroc who made of McDonald's a nation-wide, and subsequently world-wide, fast food empire. He was a milkshake machine salesman when he visited the brothers' restaurant in 1954. Thinking they had made a mistake in ordering eight of his mixers he drove there to demonstrate that the machine could produce five milkshakes at one time. He was astounded by what he saw. Realizing that the success of the store could be replicated at road intersections in many towns, he talked with the McDonald brothers about franchising the business. They, however, already had three Cadillacs and a huge house, and could not conceive of wanting more. Kroc persuaded them to sell him the franchising rights and, seven years later, bought them out.

The first of the chain was in Des Plaines, Illinois. It is now a museum. Its first mascot was Speedee McDonald, a chef with a hamburger as a head. Recognizing that America was in the middle of a baby boom the marketing was designed to be attractive to children, who would then bring parents and grandparents with them. The bright colours, the play areas and (from the early 1960s) the clown Ronald McDonald were all part of this astonishingly successful strategy. Alliances with corporations in the entertainment sector, such as Disney, led to the creation of the Happy Meal (a child-sized portion of food with a toy). The result of such targetting is that McDonald's is not only the world's biggest handler of beef and potatoes, it is also the largest distributor of toys. Ninety-six per cent of American children are able to identify Ronald McDonald – only Santa Claus scores higher.

Citizens of the UK, where the first McDonald's opened in 1974, eat more fast food than any other nationality in Europe. However it is also here that the criticism of the corporation has been strongest. A group of activists started to distribute a leaflet headed 'What's wrong with McDonald's?' It claimed that the food damaged health, and that the company exploited its workers and children. It claimed also that its meat suppliers used intensive farming practices that involved the mistreatment of animals, and its use of packaging threatened the destruction of the rain forest and increased poverty in the developing world. In 1990 McDonald's sued five members of the group, two of whom unexpectedly decided to fight the case in court. After 313 days 'the McLibel case', which had become the longest trial in English legal history, came to an end. In what was a public relations catastrophe for the corporation the judge ruled that their advertising was exploitative of children, that promoting their products as nutritious was deceptive, that their wages were low, and that suffering was involved in the rearing and slaughtering of animals used in their food. The defendants Helen Steel and Dave Morris were fined £60,000 because they had failed to prove some of their other assertions, but that fact was largely overlooked when the media treated the result as a heroic victory for the pair, standing up to a multinational 'bully' which had even used spies to infiltrate the group that circulated the leaflets.

Further criticism has been quieter, but equally damaging.

In 2002 the artists Jake and Dinos Chapman, who are among the wildly successful Young British Artists, exhibited what appeared to be 'primitive trophies and initiation masks from the former colonial regions of Camgib, Seirf and Ekoc'.[10] Brilliantly carved masks that could worthily be displayed in the African galleries of the British Museum were revealed, on closer inspection, to be wooden hamburgers fringed with raffia or fetish objects carved with golden arches. In attacking globalization for its adulteration of culture they produced work that was beautiful, funny, and yet profoundly melancholy.

A more analytical critique was provided by Eric Schlosser in *Fast Food Nation*, an unlikely best-seller that took a scalpel to junk food and ruthlessly dissected McDonald's' employment practices, the conditions under which its food is grown and prepared, and its impact on the health of the world. Cumulatively his evidence was devastating:

> The low price of a fast food hamburger does not reflect its real cost – and should. The profits of the fast food chains have been made possible by losses imposed on the rest of society. The annual cost of obesity alone is now twice as large as the fast food industry's total revenues. The environmental movement has forced companies to curtail their pollution, and a similar campaign must induce the fast food chains to assume responsibility for their business practices and minimise their harmful effects . . . The executives who run the fast food industry are not bad men. They are businessmen. They will sell free-range, organic, grass-fed hamburgers if you demand it. They will sell whatever sells at a profit.[11]

And there were signs that damage had been done. In the

final quarter of 2002 McDonald's recorded a loss of $343 million – its first ever loss in six decades. Shares fell to an eight-year low in March 2003. The company responded by closing over five hundred restaurants and pulling out of three countries altogether. However, they also responded in more unexpected ways – by introducing to the menu items that were perceived as more nutritious, such as a penne salad with chicken, tomato, spinach and basil, and a Happy Meal Fruit Bag. The corporation started quietly buying up chains that have a reputation for serving high quality food, including stakes in the upmarket sandwich chains Aroma and Pret à Manger. Eric Schlosser comments: 'The future of fast food is fresh, quality food and McDonald's knows it . . . Changing menus and investing in quality restaurants that do not bear their name makes sense.'[12]

All of which leaves Paul and me standing on the pavement of City Road, heads swivelling from north to south, reflecting that the contrast could hardly be greater between a restaurant that requires you to book a table three months in advance, and a restaurant whose customers enter on impulse because they happen to be hungry. It is the contrast that lies behind the Naked Chef's own plea: 'Don't eat to live, but live to eat.' The sociologist Margaret Visser unsettled a previous generation with her investigation into the history, mythology and production methods of staple foods:

Food is 'everyday' – it has to be, or we would not survive for very long. But food is never just something to eat . . . For most of human history we have spent a much longer portion of our lives worrying about food, and plotting, working, and fighting to obtain it . . . As soon as we can count on a food supply we start to civilise ourselves. We echo the preferences and principles of our culture in the way we treat our food . . . Food – what is chosen from the possibilities available, how it is presented, how it is eaten, with whom and when, and how much time is allotted to cooking and eating it – is one of the means by which a society creates itself and acts out its aims and fantasies. Changing (or unchanging) food choices and presentation are part of every society's tradition and character. Food shapes us and expresses us even more definitively than our furniture or houses or utensils do.[13]

The world's oldest surviving image of a meal is on a lapis-lazuli cylinder seal discovered in the royal tombs of Ur, in what is now Iraq. Dating from about 2600 BC it depicts a meal in the palace of Queen Shub-ad. The guests, seated on low stools, are being offered beakers of wine while servants fan them and a harpist plays. It was in this town, and probably in this culture, that Abraham was born. And it is from him that we get the first glimpse in the Bible that shared food is an appropriate context in which to acknowledge the presence of God. Control of the food supply meant military superiority and it was in response to the capture of his nephew Lot in a war between rival warlords, and their attempt to starve his clan into submission, that Abraham went to battle. Victorious but magnanimous, Abraham was sought out by Melchizedek, the high priest of a Jerusalem-based religion that worshipped the God who is recognizably the same creator God whom Abraham, the Jews and now the Christians worship. Melchizedek pronounced God's blessing on Abraham and it was celebrated in a shared meal of bread and wine – the first pairing in the Bible of the staple foods that are now at the heart of Christian worship.[14]

Abraham himself was the host of a meal for mysterious strangers, which the Bible interprets as a direct meeting with God. With travel hazardous and the provision of food precarious, hospitality was considered a prime duty among God's people – both the Hebrews and the early Christians. 'Do not forget to entertain strangers,' insisted one of the New Testament writers, probably alluding to Abraham, 'for by so doing some people have entertained angels without knowing it.'[15] Jesus himself depended heavily on the food and drink he was offered by others, and he encouraged his disciples to deduce whether or not people were responding to his gospel from the way they were welcomed and fed in their homes.[16] Out of this grew a Christian tradition of hospitality in imitation of the generosity of God. In the sixth century St Benedict spelled it out in the rule of life he wrote for the monastic order he had founded: 'Let all visitors who chance to arrive be welcomed as if it were Christ himself.'

The social and religious significance of food, although it is by no means exclusive to Christianity, is very evident in the Bible and through all the Jewish and Christian centuries. The supply of food was seen as an expression of God's goodness, and the whole community was to share in it. It was to be safe, nutritious and palatable, and laws that governed what could and could not enter the food chain were designed to maintain society's health. Shared meals were a vital part of family and neighbourhood cohesion. A welcome to a meal could signal forgiveness: when Joseph realized that for the first time in many years he and all the brothers who had abused him were together in one room his initial command was, 'Serve the food!'[17] And the way it was served was always indicative of the esteem in which host and guest held each other: in Jesus' story of a father lavishly welcoming home his wayward son, the older brother complains that he has never been offered so much as a scraggy goat.[18] By Jesus' time Roman practices had become standard, and formal meals for someone of his status were taken reclining on couches, arranged on three sides of a low table. Eating from communal dishes by dipping bread into them emphasized the sociable nature of the occasion, with food being passed from hand to hand in much the same way that it is recognized as a compliment to offer a friend one of your gorgeous, plump, crisp, salty chips.

Grain for bread, wine and olive oil in which to cook vegetables were the staple commodities. Meat was available only to the rich and (unless you happened to live on the coast) so was fish. Of course, for the labouring classes it was always different. With no time to eat breakfast before the working day began, they carried loaves, cheese and figs to eat on the move. Women, or the servants of wealthier households, took their meals at great speed, working around the needs of others. The poor managed as best they could.

It was precisely this division between the way the relatively rich and poor ate that gave rise to one of the most significant developments in Christian worship in its early years. Among Jesus' final instructions to his followers was to remember him through eating – not through a prayer, nor a book, nor an act of worship, but through the most fundamental action known to humankind. And the foods he chose were not special. They were the staple foods that happened to be at hand as he ate a traditional Jewish meal with his friends on the night before he died – bread and wine.

To eat together and, in fellowship with one another, find fellowship with God was one of the great delights of the church in Jerusalem in the years after Jesus' resurrection. 'They broke bread in their homes and ate together with glad and sincere hearts,' the New Testament records,

'praising God and enjoying the favour of all the people.'[19]
This kind of meal later became known as a love feast, or
agapé, and culminated in sharing bread and wine as Jesus
had taught. However, the egalitarian nature of Christian
faith was bringing together people who had not been used
to eating in each others' company. Rich and poor, slaves
and masters, were supposed to dip bread in the same dish.
It was an uncomfortable social mix, and tensions revealed
themselves. In Corinth for instance, different groups were
insisting on eating different foods, wealthier believers were
separating themselves and their dishes from poorer people,
and large quantities of alcohol were creating an atmosphere
that was not conducive to ending the meal with a reverent
reflection on the life and teaching of Jesus. Such an open
and shared act of worship was generating other problems
as well – those who had maverick theological beliefs were
bringing confusion to an event that was supposed to affirm
that Jesus was Lord. 'These men are blemishes at your love
feasts, eating with you without the slightest qualm,' protested Jude, the writer of one of the New Testament epistles.[20]

In response Paul wrote to the church at Corinth insisting that the fun of the shared meal and the solemn rite of
remembering Jesus should be kept separate. The urging,
pleading and warning (the Naked Chef method) were not
working in a church that now had many congregations and
variations. If the Church was to become global, control and
conformity (the McDonald's method) had to take their
place. Prayers with orthodox theology were composed, a
liturgical sequence was laid down, complete forms of
service were devised and, most significantly, the quantity of
bread and wine by which Jesus was to be remembered was
reduced to a bite and a sip – a symbolic rather than an
actual meal. From the churches of Syria the text of an
instruction book for Christian practice written in about

150, the *Didache*, has survived, stressing orderliness and unity:

> On Sunday, the Lord's own day, come together, break bread and carry out the eucharist . . . Begin with the chalice: 'We give thanks to thee, our Father, for the holy Vine of thy servant David, which thou hast made known to us through they servant Jesus.' Let all the people say, 'Glory be to thee, world without end.' Then over the particles of bread: 'We give thanks to thee, our Father, for the life and knowledge thou hast made known to us through thy servant Jesus.' Let all the people say, 'Glory be to thee, world without end. As this broken bread, once dispersed over the hills, was brought together to become one loaf, so may thy church be brought together from the ends of the earth into thy Kingdom.'[21]

Although the times and means and reasons are lost, somewhere along the way the celebratory and shared Lord's Supper became the atomized and individual Eucharist.

The way we live, the way we eat, and the way we worship will always be inextricably linked. The early Roman Republic, local and idealistic, was fed by its citizen farmers; the Roman Empire, vast and globalizing, was fed by its slaves. Jamie Oliver's fifteen; Ray Kroc's 1.5 million. The *agapé* meal in Jerusalem; the world-wide communion.

'I have another idea,' said Paul as we looked for a last time through the windows of the oversubscribed restaurant. 'Why don't we both contribute to the comparison between Ronald McDonald and the Naked Chef? Instead of eating at Fifteen, you go home via Sainsbury's and cook the recipe for chilli con carne from *Happy Days with the Naked Chef*.'

'So what's your contribution?'

'I'll pay virtually nothing, and get the food quickly and

effortlessly – like a customer in McDonald's. That's how we make sure the comparison is fair!'

And that, believe it or not, is how I come to be weeping as I chop chillies on a May evening. I am not enjoying this at all. I feel coerced into cooking for a teenager with an appetite the size of a small nation. I haven't got the required cumin seeds (I don't even know what cumin seeds are). I haven't got the right equipment to 'blitz' the ingredients (hence the chopping and the streaming eyes). The phone goes three times with matters that I didn't really need to be bothered with. I drop the yoghurt on the floor and only just have enough for 'a big blob' on each portion.

Tense and frustrated I put the food on the table. Paul has unplugged the phone and stuffed the end of the cable into a pot plant, which makes me grin. I realize that I have forgotten to 'serve it with loads of fresh crusty bread' so I rush back into the kitchen and slice up a loaf. As I do so I hear a cork popping out of a wine bottle in the other room. I really hope that Paul has opened a red one, because there are going to be 'some serious flavours' to compete with.

I go back to the table and put the chunks of baguette in the centre next to the Merlot. It goes quiet. The smell is pukka. Paul and I look at the bread and wine for a moment. Then for some reason that I cannot explain my mouth turns upward into an unstoppable smile. Paul laughs at me. I raise my eyebrows in the way I always do when I am suggesting we say grace. He nods his head like he always does. We thank God for the food.

Notes

1 Jamie Oliver, *Happy Days with the Naked Chef*, Michael Joseph, 2001.
2 Jamie Oliver, *The Return of the Naked Chef*, Michael Joseph 2000.

3 *The Naked Chef*, series 1, BBC2, 11 April 2000.

4 *The Observer*, 16 April 2000.

5 *The Guardian*, 5 December 2002.

6 *The Guardian*, 24 December 2001.

7 George Ritzer, *The McDonaldization of Society*, Pine Forge Press, 1996.

8 Ray Kroc, quoted in John F. Love, *McDonald's: Behind the Arches*, Bantam Books, 1995.

9 *Hamburgers in Harare*, SBS, May 2000.

10 White Cube Gallery, November 2002 – try reversing the spelling!

11 Eric Schlosser, *Fast Food Nation*, Houghton Mifflin, 2002, Penguin 2002.

12 Interviewed by John Arlidge, *Observer Food Magazine*, April 2003.

13 Margaret Visser, *Much Depends on Dinner: The Extraordinary History and Mythology, Allure and Obsessions, Perils and Taboos of an Ordinary Meal*, Penguin, 1989.

14 Genesis 14:11–20.

15 Hebrews 13:2.

16 Luke 10:5–12.

17 Genesis 43:31.

18 Luke 15:25–30.

19 Acts 2:46, 47.

20 Jude 12.

21 *Didache 14*, *Early Christian Writings*, translated by M. Staniforth, Penguin, 1968.

II

The Flower-covered Lamp-post

When you die your heart will stop beating. After that it will take about a minute for your breathing to come to an end, finishing with one last, rattling exhalation of breath. The muscles of your body will be extremely tense, but they will begin to relax from that point, which means that your bladder will empty itself.

Half an hour after your death the colour will drain from your skin. Your eyeballs will begin to sink. Your temperature will cool at about one degree per hour.

After four hours your body will begin to stiffen. It will start with your face and then spread down your torso. This effect (called rigor mortis) will be slower if suffocation was the cause of your death; faster if you died running, falling or from an electric shock.

After twenty-four hours your body will have cooled to room temperature, or the temperature of your environment if you are unfortunate enough to die outdoors. Your skin will take on a red-green tinge. At this stage the effects of rigor mortis will be reversed, starting with your toes and ending with your face. Fluid will leak from your orifices. You will begin to smell of rotting meat.

Two days later your hair and nails will still be growing. Gas will start to accumulate in your body and large red blisters will form on your skin.

Unless you are cremated your hair, nails and eventually

skin will come loose three weeks after your death. As they split, insects, maggots and then worms will start to eat your muscles and fat. The water locked in the body (about twenty gallons of it) will turn into a thick liquid and seep out. This will begin the process of reducing you to a . . .

I can't go on!

This is quite the most revolting thing I have ever written. But the only thing that shocks me about writing it is that I didn't find the information from researching medical text books. I learnt most of these things from the television – from *Silent Witness*, *Quincy* and several other television dramas in which criminal pathologists use what they have discovered during an autopsy to solve murders despite the most devious efforts of the killers to disguise their involvement. I have learnt the mechanics of death through entertainment!

It is inconceivable that a book like this would have contained such a blunt beginning to a chapter ten years ago. It is altogether more likely that a chapter about the way we mourn would have started by acknowledging death as the last taboo. It might have noted ruefully that while the Victorians talked openly about death but never about sex, society in the second half of the twentieth century rejoiced in talking about sex but kept death an unmentionable secret. However, in the twenty-first century the death taboo died.

It seems that, at present, nothing can satisfy our curiosity about what it means to be dead. In an East London art gallery a show called *Body Worlds: the Anatomical Exhibition of Real Human Bodies* extended its run again and again throughout 2002. The German anatomist Professor Günther von Hagen has perfected a process called 'plastination' by which human cadavers can be preserved to give them an unprecedentedly authentic appearance. Flayed, dissected, cross-sectioned and displayed in lifelike poses, these people (all of whom gave permission for their bodies to be used in this way) make a disquieting spectacle. One man, for example, is sculpted so that he is holding his own skin. Another leaps, every skinless muscle and sinew stretched in tension, to stop a football in a goal mouth. A woman, flayed to reveal every perfectly positioned organ, rides a similarly peeled and preserved horse. The actual presence of these people, stripped of life, both repels and transfixes. Has their dignity been violated by macabre manipulation, or has their personhood been honoured in art? Or is that distinction irrelevant when a sign outside the Atlantis Gallery boasted: 'Over ten million visitors world-wide'.

Hagen, whose gifts as an anatomist are as nothing compared with his gifts as a self-publicist, challenged both the law and the conscience of the land by performing a public autopsy in November 2002. In front of a live audience of two hundred and a television audience of over a million the professor dissected and discussed the corpse of a man who had specified in his will that his body was to be used for the advancement of medical education. A bluster of outraged comment followed in the newspapers, but no prosecution. The novelist Fay Weldon was roused to write: 'The very idea of cutting up a body in public is revolting. It is the New Obscenity.' But the run of the exhibition was extended by three months to cope with the renewed queues under the slogan 'London's most controversial immigrants are being sent home. Make sure you see them before they go.' Many critics agreed. 'Take your children,' urged *Time Out*'s art critic Sarah Kent. Professor Hagen insisted that his actions were a revival of a seventeenth-century tradition of public autopsies for serious education and existential enlightenment. He wore his trademark homburg hat throughout!

Death has become part of our fantasy life. In bookshops, murder mysteries dominate the table of best-sellers. On the television, series set in hospitals (both fictional and real) have become prime-time mainstays. In cinemas, good-looking American teenagers die in hideous ways as members of the audience jolt in their seats. It is, one might think, a return to the years before 1868 when death was staged in out-of-town arenas as a spectacle to which thousands of people, regardless of age, gender or class, flocked for a day out. But public executions were different. Criminals refused to die attractively. They kicked and bled and choked and blasphemed and shat as they died. It was not the London Dungeon with its emergency exits and orderly queues; it was real. In the twenty-first century recreational death is packaged in such a way that we can shiver without retching. It is distant and fascinating. It has as much to do with the facts of death as a pork chop, neatly presented in a polystyrene tray on a supermarket shelf, has to do with an abattoir.

But the truth remains. Within more or less eighty years of learning the facts of life all of us find out, willingly or not, the facts of death. For the 806 women who die in Britain every day the truth is most likely to catch up with them in their eighty-first year; for the 730 men in their seventy-fifth. But a fact it is, whether you are Queen Elizabeth the Queen Mother or Niamh Sullivan.

The Queen Mother died peacefully in her sleep on 30 March 2002. Her funeral service took place ten days later and she was buried in the George VI memorial chapel, part of St George's Chapel in Windsor Castle. Her coffin is next to that of her husband in a vault under a black ledger stone on which their names and dates are inscribed. Everything about the chapel inclines visitors to quiet. There is an altar on which is a Celtic cross made from perspex. The stained-glass windows designed by Sir John Piper let in a cool blue light. Wrought-iron gates separate the chapel from the body of the church, and on them is a panel which quotes words of Christian reassurance that George VI used in a radio broadcast to the nation on Christmas Day as the realities of being at war took hold in 1939:

> I said to the man who stood at the gate of the year, 'Give me a light that I may tread safely into the unknown.' And he replied, 'Go out into the darkness, and put your hand in to the hand of God. That shall be to you better than a light, and safer than a known way.'[1]

On television I watched thousands of people line the streets of London to see the funeral procession pass by. It was a subdued but spectacular day out. And as television reporters interviewed people in the crowd, enquiring what it meant to them to be witnesses at the memorial service for a lady they had never known, I willed one of them to ask: 'And when did you last visit your grandparents?' No one asked.

It was that single thought which led to me meeting the friends of Niamh Sullivan. Realizing that, fifteen years after the death of my grandfather I had never visited his grave, I went in search of it. It was not difficult to remember the location of the memorial garden where he and his wife, who died ten years before him, had their cremated ashes interred. But I couldn't find the grave among the thousands of memorial plates, each horizontal and precisely the same size, laid in an absolutely regular way in the grass. Next to each plate is a hole into which a potted plant can be lowered (a polite notice discourages cut flowers because of the difficulty of maintaining order as the flowers fade and their plastic wrappings become litter). An unexpectedly large number of graves have plants beside them, which means that the garden is very colourful.

I found my grandparents' grave on my second visit, and beside it a white heather. The words on the tarnished metal plate give their names, Kathleen and Stanley Liddelow, and the dates of their birth and death. Then there are two confident phrases: 'United together with Jesus' and 'In God's presence there is joy for evermore, Psalm 16:11'. What struck me most was the similarity between my grandparents' grave and every other one of the thousands in the garden – each identical in size, material and style of lettering. As they grew older my grandparents' desire to conform grew. They hated to stand out in a crowd. In his last years my grandfather, anxious not to be a burden, repeatedly asked, 'Have I done the right thing?' In death they are tidy, orderly, unproblematic. They have done the right thing.

Niamh Sullivan died on a treacherous piece of road in South London on 23 June 2002. She was seventeen.[2] In the early hours of Sunday morning, after celebrating the end of the exam season in a nightclub, she said goodbye to her boyfriend on the bus. At the bus stop she was within sight of her home, but a passing vehicle left the road (apparently – the details are unclear and no driver has been identified) and struck her.

Niamh's grave is about one hundred metres from that of my grandparents. A permanent plate had not yet been put in place when I visited, but a copper-coloured plastic one bore her name and dates. It was by accident of my needing to visit twice that I met three of her friends, who told me her story. She loved to dance, they told me, and had been recalled to a second round of auditions for *Popstars*, a 'reality TV' programme creating a girl band and a rival boy band. She was kind, gregarious, and the best gymnast of her school. And she was a stylish dresser. She had no time for the magazines which coerced young people into dressing in a particular way, but instead put her clothes together in imaginative ways on a limited budget to make a unique impression.

Tentatively, because their sadness was still evident, I asked Niamh's friends to show me her grave. They did, then added, 'But this isn't her real memorial.' Frustration emerged. They evidently felt that their friend had been let down by the church's provision for mourning her. The service at the crematorium had taken place so quickly after Niamh's death that there had been no time to organize for it to be an occasion to which all her friends could contribute. The duty clergyman who took the service (for whom this was possibly one of several funerals that day) did not know her and referred to her as 'our sister' throughout. Her friends assume that he was not confident about pronouncing her Celtic name correctly and so avoided it. They did not take comfort in the prescribed words of the service, repeated day after day in memory of so many kinds of people (but rarely someone so young). Niamh was unique, they felt, and the service had not recognized that. Nobody had been 'allowed to cry'. The only part of the funeral in which they had recognized her personality was in the choice of music: Robbie Williams singing 'Angel'. And they were scornful of the functional plastic plate which temporarily marked out the place at which her ashes are interred – one among so many identical plots.

I was curious about what they meant about her 'real memorial' and they took me to see it. A lamp-post near where she lived and died was covered with flowers from knee-height to well above the head. Some were plastic, bound to the upright with tape. Others were real, but had withered in their wrappings over the weeks. There were two teddy bears, a string of beads, ballet shoes, a photograph and several hand-written cards and notes: 'To our daughter, sister and aunt'; 'Every day your thoughts are in mine'; 'Living all peacefully up there'; 'You are so special and I miss you more than I can say'. As soon as we arrived the three young people began tidying the flowers and removing rubbish from the area. They were taken by surprise to discover that a cutting from a newspaper had been added showing a photograph of Holly Wells and Jessica Chapman, two young schoolgirls who had been murdered in Soham, Cambridgeshire. It had been neatly cut and pasted on card with the words, 'Playing together in heaven.' After a discussion they decided to remove it and place it somewhere more appropriate.

'Was Niamh a Christian?' I asked. Oh yes, came the reply. 'Did she go to a church of any kind?' No. 'What did she do to express her faith?' The three looked at each other and there was a pause before one of them answered, 'She was a Christian like Princess Diana.'

At once the lamp-post had a context. During September 1997 the image of Diana, Princess of Wales, took on an iconic status in the weeks following her death. It was bound into bouquets, displayed in windows, superimposed on merchandise and, yes, attached to lamp-posts. Carpets of flowers, each with a message that hinted at an impossible personal acquaintance, appeared in many places. None of them were religious sites. Rather, flowers were placed in Paris at the entrance to the tunnel where her car crashed fatally, at Kensington Palace, and at other sites associated with her life. Books of condolence were signed in churches, but also in palaces, libraries and supermarkets (where it was possible to shop and be sad at the same time, which seems particularly in keeping with the life of Diana). The floral shrines became revered in an unprecedented way – a thief who stole a bunch was sentenced to four weeks in jail.

When the task of removing them from Kensington Palace inevitably came round, the public was assured that they were to be composted and thus recycled into new growth.

It seems to have been the response to the tragedy at Hillsborough football stadium in April 1989 which first allowed a large-scale and emotional display of grief to escape from the churches and find expression in public places. Following the death of nearly one hundred spectators, mainly Liverpool supporters, a huge carpet of scarves and flowers was placed in Anfield Stadium. Although the practice of leaving flowers at the sites of fatal accidents predates this, there had never before been a spontaneous decision to mark a tragedy in a way which made the traditional Christian rites seem secondary. Four years later in the same part of England the murder of two-year-old Jamie Bulger provoked a similar national grief, and the site where his body was found was heaped with flowers. And in March 1996 the killing of sixteen children and their teacher at a primary school in Dunblane, Scotland, became a focus for the nation openly to mourn, with politicians visiting to lay wreaths and reflect on what society should learn from such a trauma.

The funeral of Diana though, with its massed displays of anguish on the streets, has served to make a quite different way of marking death acceptable. 'A unique service for a unique person' was the way the Dean of Westminster Abbey described it. And indeed it was unique, with Sir Elton John's entirely secular *Candle in the Wind* performed alongside Sir John Tavener's profoundly religious *Song for Athene* in which words from the Bible and Shakespeare resound with alleluias. And outside the cathedral the vast crowd, some of them distraught, marked Diana's death with their own rituals – lighting candles, writing messages, clinging to each other in silence. At the height of the service they applauded. The Christian tradition of the centuries made appropriate to a secular saint with homespun and personal ceremonies. Outside a cathedral in London, or next to a busy road in Croydon.

In her book *Vigor Mortis*, a superb analysis of how society has tamed the last taboo, Kate Berridge draws attention to the irony that, in the UK in 2002, approximately nine out of ten funerals are conducted with Christian rites despite the fact that approximately one out of ten people go to church. She is not surprised by the need for people to make their farewells to those they have loved in a personalized way because they find it impossible to understand the constraints of Christian heritage. 'For example, "Our Dear Mum" was vetoed in one parish where the authorities thought "Our Dear Mother" more suitable.'[3] She points to the rise of new secular rituals, such as the release of helium-filled balloons (which, like flowers, are colourful but short-lived), websites on which visitors can add messages to go alongside photographs and memories, or applause as the coffin passes from view: 'There is no legal requirement to go to a church or crematorium at all . . . Hands clasped in clapping, not in prayer, is a good vignette of modern death.'

Some aspects of the grieving process persist beyond reason. The flowers which feature in almost every funeral rite, Christian or secular, were originally part of the procedure for a completely practical reason – the need to disguise the increasing smell of the corpse. However, the tradition has persisted long after undertakers and chemicals have removed the need. The exaggeratedly slow pace of the hearse (so marked that it has its own adjective, funereal) was also essential in centuries gone by because a candlelit procession had to go slowly in order to keep the flames alight, but the habit has survived the invention of the petrol engine.

The most notable changes in the way we mourn have been shaped by changes in the spiritual beliefs held by the majority of the nation. Until the sixteenth century most people were buried in unmarked graves unless they were from the nobility. Because Roman Catholic belief was that the prayers of the living could influence the eternal destiny of the dead, the emphasis was not on the position of the body but on the location of the soul. With the new developments in theological understanding that came with the Reformation, the emphasis shifted and the need of those left behind to have a place at which to focus their grief became central. The wording on gravestones became more elaborate and personal, and the images changed to match the pervading belief. Sixteenth-century memorials feature bones and skulls, confronting the visitor with the reality of bodily death and reminding them to pray for the soul of the deceased person (or pay for someone else to say the prayers). But alongside Reformation theology that it is God's grace alone which has won believers eternal life, a new imagery of angels and the welcoming arms of Jesus appeared. It grew increasingly sentimental throughout the Victorian age. One feature that did not change was the shame of dying without enough funds put aside for a decent Christian burial, which became a real burden upon poor people.

The belief in a literal resurrection of the body (and the superstitions which surrounded it, such as the one that people buried on the south side of a cemetery would rise to eternal life before those in other parts) made burial the only logical Christian option. Cremation was illegal in the UK until 1884. But literal interpretations of spiritual truths were running out – and so was space in a small island. The Cremation Society fought a long and eventually successful campaign to persuade the nation of its preference in terms of hygiene. A Mrs Pickersgill of Woking, Surrey, was the pioneer of a system which in the UK now accounts for the departure of 72 per cent of the population.

Victorians felt a powerful pressure to conform to an appropriate form of behaviour after a bereavement. Black mourning dress made it obvious that a woman had been widowed, and she was required to wear this for two years, with the severity of the style relaxing slightly every six months to denote the passing of time. There were funeral tea services, black-edged writing paper and mourning jewellery. However, social constraints forbade women from expressing their grief with emotions – it was not common for them even to attend their husbands' funerals until the 1890s.

It was the First World War that accounted for the most dramatic shift in attitudes. Those who fought in the trenches witnessed death and the treatment of the dead in such a brutal form that nothing in the mourning rituals (or for many, the Christianity faith itself) could accommodate the horror of what they had seen. For millions of widows there was no body to grieve over. Memory and remembrance became, unavoidably, more important in the mourning process than the presence of remains. When in 1920 the unidentifiable body of a soldier was buried in Westminster Abbey with state honours to stand for all whose place of burial was unknown, queues stretched for seven miles to place flowers near 'the Tomb of the Unknown Warrior'. It was to be seventy-seven years before there was a comparable occasion.

Death by gas or mortar or mud has a hideous anonymity to it, and after the major battles of Ypres and the Somme three-quarters of the casualties were either unidentifiable or lost. A government decision that remains were not to be repatriated led to the creation of vast cemeteries in France and Belgium. Tyne Cot, the British War Cemetery near Ypres is the largest with twelve thousand graves. Rank after rank of identical white headstones stand in rows in the green grass as if they were still subject to military drill. Their uniformity – 76 cm high and 8 cm wide – was deliberate. It was a design of Frederic Kenyon, the director of the British Museum. The nameless inscription on many, 'A Soldier of the Great War Known unto God', was composed by Rudyard Kipling, whose own son John is among them.

Death needed new rites. Mourning dress was abandoned because the morale of troops on leave could not be sustained when there were constant reminders of the vast numbers of bereaved people. The memory of people became more significant than the site of their burial. New rituals were developed and endure – the two minutes of silence on Armistice Day, the wearing of poppies, and the honouring of war memorials.

However, the Victorian need to conform (in death as in so many other things) survived and is still in evidence in the absolute regularity of cemeteries such as Greenlawns Memorial Garden, where my grandparents lie, twelve graves along and three graves up from Niamh Sullivan.

But there is a world of difference between the life of faith which characterized Kathleen and Stanley's generation and that in which Niamh danced. Theirs was a society in which they wanted to be measured by their souls. Dying in absolute assurance of meeting the God of love, the fact that their memorial is identical to a thousand others is insignificant. For those of us who love them it is the anticipation of meeting them again through the grace of a God in whose presence 'is fullness of joy' that keeps them in our memory. But for a secular generation with a diminished concept of the soul, where people perceive themselves as defined by their own bodies and personalities, the need for individuality in memorials has become increasingly necessary. And it is this which gives rise to customized funeral services, websites of virtual cemeteries, environmentally aware woodland burials in plots marked by the planting of a tree, and informal clothes at ceremonies lively with colour and personal recollections.

And the flower-covered lamp-post! As well as Niamh's there are five to which I could drive in a matter of minutes. They are respected, carefully maintained and unique to the memory of Noel who died on his motorbike on the A212, to Sally who was tragically killed outside a South London school, and to three others whose names I do not know but beside whose memorials I have prayed.

One desultory Tuesday morning at the end of the last century I read that the world's six billionth human had been born. The newspapers reported that there are now more humans alive on the planet than have previously existed in the whole of history. The living outnumber the dead. Niamh Sullivan, who wanted to be famous, and my grandparents, who hated to stand out in a crowd, all find themselves in a minority.

Long live their memory!

Notes

1 Minnie Louise Haskins, *Desert*, 1908.
2 At the request of her family, this is not her real name.
3 Kate Berridge, *Vigor Mortis: The end of the death taboo*, Profile Books, 2002.

12

The Cross

This is the actress Julia Stiles, star of the Hollywood movie *10 Things I Hate About You*, speaking about the crucifix she wears around her neck: 'It's plastic. It's an ode to Madonna. Actually, my dog chewed it. It's really bad. I let my dog chew on Jesus Christ's feet.'[1]

MADONNA? Good grief! We are not talking about the Blessed Virgin Mary here! What kind of religion inspires someone to wear ancient, sacred symbols to venerate Madonna?

'I'm, like, from a generation of kids that don't know what to believe in, so we don't believe anything at all.'[2]

Madonna Ciccone is the actress and singer who, by cleverly packaging and promoting a modest talent, has risen to become one of the most famous women in the world. In 1989 she performed her hit song 'Like a Prayer' in Rome wearing so little that the crucifix around her neck was unmistakable. The stage performance mirrored the video of the song, which featured Madonna writhing in front of a black, Christ-like figure on a cross that wept blood. Outrage and threats from the Vatican led Pepsi Corporation to withdraw sponsorship of the tour. The singer, however, pocketed five million dollars and watched her album rise to number one. She seems never to have done anything in her professional career the impact of which was not carefully calculated, so to protest innocence into a microphone so close to the Vatican was unconvincing: 'I don't make fun of Catholicism; I deeply respect Catholicism. When I was growing up I was religious in a passionate way. Jesus Christ was like a movie star, my favourite idol of all . . . Crucifixes are sexy because there's a naked man on them.'[3]

With or without Madonna's help crucifixes are indeed sexy at the start of the twenty-first century. Is it possible that the central symbol of the Christian faith has regained its power to excite and offend? Perhaps that depends on whether it is worn iconically or ironically. The Vatican, through its missionary agency Fides, was predictable in its disapproval, but unpredictable in its decision to name names:

> There is a spreading fashion of wearing crosses decorated with diamonds and other precious stones. Jennifer Aniston wears a cross of precious stones, model Naomi Campbell has an enormous collection of jewel-studded crosses, and actress Catherine Zeta Jones wears a gold and diamond cross. This mania is incomprehensible . . . Is it relevant to the spirit of the gospels to spend thousands to buy a sacred symbol of Christianity and then in an unchristian manner forget those who suffer and die of hunger in the world?[4]

The *Daily Mirror* lost no time in joining the condemnation. The next day it reported 'Vatican cross', giving it an excuse to print ravishing photographs of the three celebrities under the headline 'The Unholy Trinity', each of them brazenly displaying the crucified Jesus between their holy duality!

More offensive in every way is the cross that has been

scratched on a wall in Rome for seventeen centuries. Next to the cross is the image of a young man with his hand raised in a gesture of worship still recognizable in many churches today. The words scraped out underneath are sour in their mockery: 'Alexamenus worships his god.' On the cross the naked Jesus can plainly be seen, viewed from behind. His head has been replaced by a donkey's head. It is the earliest image of Jesus that has survived – indelible graffiti the sole intention of which was to shock and wound.

Until relatively recently it was thought that several centuries passed before the cross was universally venerated by Christians as a sign that identified their passionate faith. Art books written thirty years ago identify the oldest decorative cross as the one on the door of the Church of Saint Sabina, built in Rome in 430: 'It is stuck away in a corner almost out of sight. [Before that] Christian art is concerned with the miracles, healings and hopeful aspects of the faith like the ascension, second coming, and the resurrection.'[5]

However, recently there have been new archaeological discoveries of burial ossuaries from the second century. So many of them are identified as Christian by a cross (as well as a fish, a star or a plough) that it is becoming accepted that the symbol was established as something to rejoice in within 150 years of Jesus' death. These early representations of the cross show it in its shortened form (like a mathematical sign for addition); the 'Latin' cross which instantly identifies Christianity today became common from the eighth century onwards.

It is easy to understand why the cross did not immediately suggest itself as a universal symbol of the Christian hope. It is not at all clear that the shape of the device for Jesus' execution was the same as the one on which he hangs

in a million churches today. It may perhaps have been a
stake to which a cross beam was attached, or scaffolding,
or even just a tree – the Romans were not fussy about the
aesthetics of capital punishment as long as the job was done
with pain and humiliation. And there were some Christian
leaders during the years when the church was organizing
itself who opposed the use of the cross as a symbol because
it had pagan associations from long before the Christian
era. Similar shapes predate Jesus in Egyptian mythology
(where it was a sign of life and has been found bearing the
words 'Ptolemy our Saviour' referring to the pharaoh who
reigned three hundred years before Christ) and in Greek
mythology (where Apollo, the god of light and healing,
carried a cross-shaped sceptre).

But by the middle of the second century, the great theo-
logian Justin was seeing the cross everywhere. Everywhere!
In . . .

> . . . all the common things that we can readily see. Ask
> yourself whether effective administration or community
> could take place anywhere in the world if there were no
> shape of the cross. You can only cross the sea when you
> make use of a sail, hanging from the cruciform mast of a
> ship. Without that shape a plough could not turn the
> earth, nor could diggers and mechanics do their work. In
> fact, the very thing that makes the human form different
> from the animals is that men and women can stand erect
> their with hands extended . . . This too shows the power
> of the form of the cross.[6]

The great power of the cross's shape is its sheer abun-
dance throughout the natural and manufactured worlds.
Like that other enduring symbol of human experience, the
circle, its attraction lies in the fact that tuned-in eyes see
crosses wherever they look. From where I sit at this

moment it calls to me from the shelves of the bookcase, the wood of the window frame, the intersections of the garden fence, even the branches of the trees. It is there at every crossroad which, since the days of the most ancient, primal religions, have been places of veneration. In the most enduring language of the world, Chinese, the ideogram for 'earth' is a cross within a square. And the Garden of Eden itself was the source of four rivers that criss-crossed and blessed with fertility all that was known of the world by the antediluvian storytellers.[7]

Its symbolism is of opposites held in tension. The circle, which has been held in awe ever since a human first lifted his head to the warmth of the sun, suggests harmony and completeness. But in contrast the cross is the scaffolding of the world, holding together its contradictions. In its meeting of vertical and horizontal it stands for the encounter of heaven and earth. Violence and peacemaking are held together in its intersection, and so are life and death themselves. At the meeting of its two formidable strokes all lines diverge, and all lines find their ending. It sends us out on a search which will finally bring us all to the same place. No wonder it has captured the human imagination for century after century.

Its paradoxes have refreshed its meaning in each century. It can bring life, when guns fall silent so that an ambulance bearing a Red Cross can reach the wounded; it can bring death, when a chalk cross on a cell door condemns a French aristocrat to the guillotine. It can repel a vampire and it can invite a kiss. It can elect a politician and reject an incorrect answer. It is the signature of a bishop and the first warning of a plague. It is formed by the hilt of a crusader's sword enabling him to pray and kill with the same implement. And Madonna must surely be aware that in her cleavage it alludes to both the virgin and the whore.

From the thirteenth century to the seventeeth century in Western Europe the crucifixion of Jesus was painted more than any other subject. In the Roman Catholic tradition statues and paintings were and are more likely to show the cross bearing the figure of Jesus, showing God identifying with humanity in suffering alongside every woman and man. In Protestant churches the cross is more likely to be displayed empty, for the Jesus who occupied it is tied by death no longer, but risen and glorified and gone where faithful humankind will follow. The birth of Jesus and the visit of Gabriel to Mary to announce her pregnancy are almost as common in art, but hanging above an altar in a candlelit church, a cross was the ideal subject-matter for the eyes of the faithful. Its compelling vertical drew an unmistakable line from the bread and wine, consecrated on the altar table, to heaven where the risen Jesus reigns. Its heart-rending horizontal is mirrored in the outstretched arms of the priest consecrating the elements. At its intersection Jesus the mediator is lifted between God and the people, his hands reaching out in pity and welcome to bring salvation to those who participate in the Eucharist blessed at his feet. And around the cross the figures witnessing his death with piety, sorrow or shame stand for each of us, allowing us to be present at the very moment his body and blood were given for the world.

In 1475 Antonello, an Italian from Messina working in Venice, painted his crucifixion.[8] It is typical in many ways of thousands of paintings of the passion of Jesus. The terrible events are taking place not outside first-century Jerusalem, but in a recognizably Italian landscape of the fifteenth century. 'This is taking place now,' Antonello is saying. 'You recognize the setting and you recognize the clothes, so understand the relevance of these piteous events to your own lives.'

In Antonello's portrayal the shape of the cross is especially striking. It imposes itself on the composition almost geometrically. Its vertical splits the picture from top to bottom, and its horizontal is precisely parallel with the horizon where a tranquil sea meets the heavens. On the cross Jesus hangs with a noble and completely calm resignation. This is in contrast to the thieves crucified on either side of him, who writhe and twist in torment. They have been executed not on crosses, but forked trees, whose curved and deformed branches increase the impression that the cross of Jesus, symmetrical and orderly, is a place where spiritual peace can be found. Antonello asks his viewers: 'What will your response be to the ever-present reality of the crucified Jesus? Are you the young man on the right, kneeling with hands clasped and eyes upturned in grateful piety? Are you Jesus' mother, slumped on the left among the skulls with her face, swollen with intolerable grief in an extremely realistic manner, turned down to the ground? Or are you the farmers and merchants, on foot or on horseback in the background, ignorantly or perhaps defiantly oblivious to the importance for their lives of the events taking place while they go about their business in the warmth of an Italian summer?'

Walking through any gallery that houses art from the centuries of the Western European tradition, it is immediately obvious that biblical subjects cease to feature in paintings as the twentieth century begins. To be fair, the significance of the cross did not completely disappear from artwork. It features prominently in memorials built after the First World War. A Maltese cross, with its four arms spiked into eight triangular points, was the first image to appear on John Logie Baird's television screen. And beside the A1, near Gateshead, Anthony Gormley's *The Angel of the North*, a distinctly earthbound angel with its outstretched aeroplane wings pleading for flight, blesses the motorist's rear-view mirror with the shape of a cross for several miles. But images of Jesus' crucifixion do not often feature in the work of major artists in the twenty-first century.

There are fine exceptions. The Scottish artist Craigie Aitchison, who is a member of the Royal Academy of Arts and a winner of the Jerwood Prize, was born in 1926. He has painted the crucifixion of Christ on many occasions. In 2003 his *Crucifixion with Dog* placed Jesus, his arms broken and angular over the horizontal of the cross, in an utterly barren setting.[9] Against a background of bleak sepia and blue, Jesus is limp and ashen. Like Antonello before him, Aitchison has placed Jesus in the landscape of the present day. But where the fifteenth-century artist portrayed the geographical landscape of his age, Aitchison has represented the derelict spiritual landscape of the present generation in which and for which Jesus is dying. A grey dog occupies the space where Mary slumped in Antonello's composition, his forlorn two-dimensional form staring up at Jesus' huge eyes. But a sliver of moon provides a distant hope, and its light shining on Christ's ginger hair gives it the sheen of a halo and illuminates the expectant face of the dog (which appears in many of Craigie Aitchison's works and seems to stand for the artist himself).

Both paintings are ravishing; neither portrayal of a disgusting way to die is shocking to present-day eyes. In both those respects they are the opposite of the compositions of the London artist Sebastian Horsley, who works in video and paint. In August 2000, before beginning work on a series of paintings of the cross, he set out to be crucified.

Rituals in which young men undergo crucifixion as an act of devotion have been taking place in the Philippines since 1961. During the week before Easter the village of San Pedro Kutud has become the stage for an event that has become notorious world-wide. In misguided attempts to twist God's arm to perform a miracle for a sick relative or a destitute farmer, Filipino men strip to loin cloths, beat themselves raw, and submit to being nailed to crosses. Thousands watch, to the delight of local hoteliers and souvenir sellers.

Accompanied by a photographer, a film-maker, and three women in blue and white robes, Horsley bribed local officials £1,000 to allow a private event to take place out of season. He was nailed to a cross, which was lifted to a vertical position. Overcome with the pain, he fainted. As he fell forward the foot support collapsed and Horsley plummeted. The organizer of the event rushed forward and caught his weight just in time to stop the nails ripping through his flesh. Later that night Horsley was overwhelmed with depression. He wrote in his diary: 'There is no question in my mind. I have been punished by a God I don't believe in, and he has thrown me off the cross for impersonating his son, for being an atheist, and for being a disaster. I have made a complete fool of myself. I am going to be a laughing stock.'

An exhibition of the framed nails, the photographs, the film, and paintings of the cross in unremitting, inky colours was turned down by almost every London art gallery. It was finally displayed at the East End gallery The Crucifix Lane Project.[10] The painted crosses, although they have faint streaks of colour that suggest human presence, are empty: 'This is not some painting of what it would appear to be crucified. It is from intimate knowledge of what it is like to go through that. And I feel this wonderful privilege that I am probably the first artist in history to do it.'[11]

The work divided critics deeply. It is difficult to explain what Horsley calls 'an orgy of rejection' in an age when corpses can be displayed as art and bodily fluids of all kinds are accepted as legitimate media in which to work sculptures. It may have been that the subject matter was too intense, or it may have been that the work was simply considered poor. Was the problem that the cross arouses too many personal passions to be treated in this way, or that its power is recognized by too few people to care?

In 1998 the International Olympic Committee, wanting to investigate the power of their logo, commissioned the London firm Sponsorship Research International to count the numbers of adults in six countries who could identify a series of symbols. In the UK, Australia, Germany, India, Japan and the United States they showed people the Olympic Games logo – five interlocking rings at least one of whose colours feature in every national flag of the world – as well as a number of comparable emblems. The rings were correctly identified by 92 per cent of the population – more than any other symbol. The golden arches of McDonald's and the yellow scallop of Shell International were both recognized by 88 per cent. The red cross and (in Muslim countries) red crescent of the international humanitarian organizations were known by 47 per cent. Those who knew that the globe nestling in olive leaves on a pale blue background belonged to the United Nations came to 36 per cent, and 28 per cent identified the World Wide Fund for Nature by its panda logo. The percentage of people who recognized the Christian cross was 54 – neither at one extreme nor the other. Critics of the research method, evidently disappointed that the cross did not register a higher percentage, suggested that the question was confusing since the cross does not represent a single organization or business like the others – it represents an ideology. They intimated that many who knew only too well that the cross is a Christian symbol failed to answer the question because the obvious answer seemed too easy. But subsequent world-wide research, for example by the American journal *Whole Earth Review*, confirms that brand logos are consistently recognized by teenagers more readily than any religious symbol.

My guess is that recognition of the Christian cross in South London is typical in this respect. Every Christmas Croydon Council arranges for some of the lights of its tower block offices to be left on overnight. It is part of an attempt to use multicoloured lighting to make Croydon a distinctive town after dark in the middle of the sprawl of otherwise indistinguishable streets of suburban London. One side of the building is illuminated in the unsurprising shape of a Christmas tree, but for the other side they have chosen the shape of a cross. It stands out for miles across the surrounding hills. It infuriates some residents, as letters to the local papers show, but others take strength from its prominence in the town. It provokes the very division that Paul anticipated when he wrote to the church that worshipped in Corinth: 'The cross is nonsense to those who are being lost; but for us who are being saved it is God's power.'[12]

Nonsensical? So the cross has seemed to some people ever since it was scrawled as graffiti on a wall in Rome.

Powerful? Its shape held before the eyes of dying people has enabled them to summon the courage to let go their final breath without fear.

Paul would have expected both attitudes. But he could surely never have foreseen it being ignored. Ignored? Yes, I suppose so! That is the destiny of all the signs of the times. They become so ubiquitous that they go unnoticed: The swoosh that is so beautifully shaped that it seems not to be a design but part of the engineering of a shoe. The bottle of water in so many hands that we forget there was recently a time when we drank in a different way. The loyalty card that is unremarkable among a dozen cards in a wallet. The faded flowers on a lamp-post that drooped so long ago that they have become invisible among the pavement debris.

Why do I want the Christian cross to be different? It is on view everywhere. That is its success. Everywhere! Why is it that I feel an urgency to shout to people, 'Notice this sign! Let it reach out and take hold of your life. Let it work its miracle'?

There beneath the cross of light shining from Croydon's office block I watch workmen – pounding and digging and shouting as they resurface the road – and I feel an urge to bellow, 'Look up! Notice how close you are to a miracle.'

In the shadow of the town-centre church, whose stone cross has perched on top of its steeple for a hundred years, I catch sight of an elderly woman – shy, sad eyes peeping from behind a curtain into the noisy street – and I feel an urge to call out, 'Look across! Notice how close you are to a miracle.'

Dressed in T-shirts on the back of which are blood-spattered Celtic crosses advertising their favourite death-metal band, I step out of the path of skateboarding teenagers – oblivious to the cold of December – and I feel an urge to shout, 'Look behind you! Notice how close you are to a miracle.'

A stone's throw from the war memorial, poppies as red as shame beneath its carved cross, I drive past a bearded man – hungry and homeless, rummaging through last night's waste in the dustbins by the Indian restaurant – and I feel an urge to cry, 'Look down the street! Notice how close you are to a miracle.'

With a gold cross hanging crooked around her neck, I walk past a woman weeping at the bus stop – on and on and embarrassingly on for who-knows-what tragedy – and I feel an urge to whisper, 'Look down! Notice how close you are to a miracle.'

And did I bellow, call, shout, cry, whisper? No, I did not. God forgive me! Instead I came home, sat at the keyboard and typed. Sad and useless and angry I typed all the things that I could have and should have, but never would have, said.

I could have said to the workmen ripping up the paving slabs, 'If men do these things when the tree is green, what will happen when it is dry?'

I could have said to the lady at the window, 'Woman here is your son. Friend, here is your mother.'

I could have said to the young guy on skates, 'This man was truly the Son of God.'

I could have said to the destitute man, 'Father forgive them, for they do not know what they are doing.'

I could have said to the woman at the bus stop, 'Today you will be with me in Paradise.'[13]

But I did not. I passed by as unnoticed as the cross. I lost my chance to say that those two simple lines, vertical and horizontal, are the sign of something astounding. Too remarkable for Christians to keep to themselves. For the cross is the sign that one Friday, some twenty centuries ago, God and humankind were momentarily at one. It happened in a way that it so complex that billions of pages of redoubtably difficult books have only inched their way toward an explanation, but so simple that two intersecting lines describe all that one needs to know. God and humankind. Vertical and horizontal. Impossible and natural. It was a miracle!

For those who accept the Christian faith that Jesus was God, walking among us as a person, the cross is the sign of the great miracle of the human era. For if it was indeed God who was walking on earth incarnate as Jesus, the most astonishing miracle is not that God should live on Easter Sunday; it is that God should die on Good Friday.

Resurrection is in God's nature. Bringing planets whirling into the life of the universe at the dawn of time is in God's nature. Creating life that grows and photosynthesises and breathes where previously there was only the dead weight of rock is in God's nature. Dragging spring flowers from the granite earth of winter is in God's nature. Bringing irrepressible life to a baby where once there was nothing but intangible love is in God's nature. He is the resurrection God.

But death is not in God's nature. It should be, for him, utterly impossible. For those who have taken hold of Jesus as God, Easter Sunday resurrection comes as no surprise; it is Good Friday death that is the miracle.

In life Jesus, God with us, achieved what a human cannot do; but in dying he has achieved what not even a god had ever been considered able to do. God has changed not only the order of things on earth, but the order of everything in the spiritual realm. If it is God who hangs on this cross, it is not an execution that we are witnessing; it is an unspeakable phenomenon. The words, 'I thirst,' speak to us not only of the pity, but of a marvel. The words, 'It is finished,' speak to us not only of the brutality, but of a wonder.

A marvel and a wonder that is a sign for all times, and which will endure those who wear it around the neck and flaunt it for a gem just as surely as it has been the salvation of those like the fifteenth-century poet William Langland who 'creep to it on knees and kiss it for a jewel'.[14]

Notes

1 *The Independent*, 13 September 2002.
2 Ibid.
3 www.madonna.ca/she_said.htm
4 Fides, Agenzia della Congregazione per l'Evangelizzazione dei Popoli, bulletin 22 May 2002.

5 Kenneth Clark, *Civilisation*, BBC Books, 1969.
6 Justin Martyr, *First Apology*, addressed to Emperor Antonius Pius, about 140.
7 Genesis 2:10–14.
8 Antonello da Messina, *Crucifixion*, Musée Royal des Beaux Arts, Antwerp, Belgium.
9 Craigie Aitchison, *Crucifixion with Dog*, 2003, Advanced Graphics, London.
10 www.crucifixlaneproject.com
11 OM Magazine, *The Observer*, 26 May 2002.
12 1 Corinthians 1:18, *Good News Bible*.
13 Luke 23:31, John 19:26, Mark 15:39, Luke 23:34, Luke 23:43.
14 William Langland, *Piers Plowman*, Passus 18 (The Harrowing of Hell).

An Empty Tomb

Where?

I have looked for the image of an empty tomb in precisely the same way in which I searched for the other signs of the times. I have leafed through magazines and peered at billboards. I have trawled the internet. I have gazed around churches. I have exasperated friends and embarrassed strangers. I have sat and watched in coffee bars; I have stood and watched on tube trains. I have whispered in libraries and shouted in nightclubs. I did not need to go far – all the signs of the times in this book came to find me.

Except an empty tomb!

As a theological concept the empty tomb is absolutely central to the Christian faith. A dead Jesus would have become a historical figure like Socrates or Confucius, revered for his wisdom, questions about whom appeared in the tense, later stages of *Who Wants to be a Millionaire?* But a Jesus who has risen from the dead is worshipped as God, and his Spirit is a living and active power in people's lives. It is the belief that the women who arrived at Jesus' tomb early on a Sunday morning found it empty that turns a philosophy into a faith. It is the empty tomb which means that the impact of Christianity reaches beyond the twenty centuries of its existence on into eternity.

So where is it?

Curiously, not only is it invisible as a sign of the times in this generation, it has never been prominent as a sign of Christian faith in any generation. The cross of Jesus' crucifixion has effortlessly become Christianity's most recognizable reference point. In advertisers' sexist terms it is easy to see why. The cross is masculine – a thrusting, potent, militant logo. The tomb is feminine – its curved hollows and uncertain shadows cannot compete.

The sole exception that the internet offers comes from Empty Tomb Witnessing Jewellery, a North American business retailing Christian merchandise, which sells a silver, two-dimensional pendant of the empty tomb to wear on a chain around your neck or ankle. On a grassy hill with three tiny crosses in the distance, a round stone has rolled aside to reveal that the occupant of the tomb is gone. Costing $12, it is part of a jewellery range that is 'inspired by God, designed by Denise Herriford'. In an exchange of e-mails she let me know:

> In my Christian walk I found that the cross upon which Christ died has been secularised – everyone is wearing them. They are just a pretty piece of jewellery . . . But the empty tomb completes our faith. I wanted to let people know that I believe in a risen Christ . . . Wearing the sign of the empty tomb lets people know exactly what I believe in and helps me to remember that I want my behaviour, attitude and life to reflect what I believe.[1]

The best evidence for how the faith was symbolized in the first Christian centuries comes from epitaphs on the tombs of those who died in the assurance that they were stepping into an eternal life in the company of Jesus Christ. The image of a fish is the most prominent in the catacombs of Rome – the huge complex of underground burial galleries excavated by Christians in the soft tufa stone outside the city. As well as a logo that could easily be scratched in the dust as a secret sign, the fish was probably an acrostic. The initial letters of the Greek words *Iesous CHristos THeou Uios Soter* spell *ICHTHUS* (fish) and they mean Jesus Christ, Son of God, Saviour. Thus a simple visual aid could also help to explain the essentials of Christian belief.

The fish sign has survived the passing of time as a mark of the presence of Christians and its appearance is nowadays the first indication that a car is likely to swerve life-threateningly into your lane on the M25.

There are other recurring symbols from the early Christian years. A shepherd carrying a lamb home across his broad shoulders referred directly to Jesus' identification of himself as 'the Good Shepherd who lays down his life for the sheep'.[2] A dove holding an olive branch referred to the story of Noah and was indicative of peace after storms and salvation after catastrophe.[3] An anchor also appears on gravestones and may have been an image of hope and security, or perhaps significant simply because the cross is unmistakable as part of the shape. By the end of the fifth century the cross had overtaken all of these in its ubiquity, but the empty tomb barely featured at all.

It continued rarely to be seen through centuries of Christian art, not only in the Western European tradition that is most familiar from art galleries, but also in African and Asian imagery. On the few occasions when the risen Jesus was painted he was often shown stepping from the tomb. One of art's defining images is Piero della Francesca's *Resurrection*, painted on the wall of the town hall in the Italian town of San Sepulcro in 1480.[4] In it Jesus towers over the sleeping soldiers. As a chilly, grey dawn steals in behind him he stands in utter triumph, his idealized muscular body as still as a statue, with one foot mounting the side of an anachronistic fifteenth-century grave. His eyes look at you, and into you, and through you, and know everything about you. C. S. Lewis points out that these are the eyes of one who has harrowed Hell.[5] They are filled with knowledge too great for a human to bear: 'If your eyes had seen what these eyes have seen . . .'

This image, spectacular and moving though it is, bears no relation to any of the biblical accounts of the circumstances of the first Easter. The great miracle of that morning was the least visual of events – the fact that the body of Jesus, the very reason the women went to the garden, was not in the tomb. How can the central image of a painting be an object which isn't there?

Crucifixion is visual, however. It is mercilessly public. That is one of the reasons it is so disgusting. And it is deafeningly surrounded by noise. Crucifixion comes with screams. It comes with cries of pain and wailing of women. It comes with hurling of abuse and vicious mockery. Its drama is hideous and explicit. It comes with earthquakes; it shivers into eclipse; it is nauseating in its rituals. And every raw, terrifying, barbaric humiliation of it is exposed and public.

Resurrection is not like that. Resurrection is not like that at all! Resurrection doesn't come with triumph, or with shouts of praise, or with exultant singing, or surrounded by adoring crowds, or with signs and wonders. Jesus Christ rose from the dead in absolute silence, in the dark of the night, with no ceremony, in the cold of a tomb, and with no witnesses. For Jesus, death was public and noisy. But . . .

> Power, but Might,
> But Life again, but Victory,
> Were hushed within the dead of night,
> The shuttered dark, the secrecy,

And all alone, alone, alone,
He rose again behind the stone.[6]

Alice Meynell's iconoclastic poem 'Easter Night' draws attention to a simple fact that theologians of the resurrection, earnestly debating whether or not the first visitors to Jesus' empty tomb prove the events to be historically accurate, miss. By the time the women came with spices, by the time the earthquake's aftershock agitated the garden, by the time the soldiers fell comatose with fright, by the time the young man in white took his seat, by the time the stone was rolled away from the mouth of the tomb . . . they had all missed it. Without an announcement of any kind, Jesus had got on with what God alone can do, and for which he needed no help. He had quietly risen from the dead.

This is the least spectacular revolution of the human era. The French Revolution was announced by the storming of the Bastille. The revolution in China began with the Long March of a million men. The Berlin Wall was torn down brick by brick in front of live television cameras. Aeroplanes flew into the Twin Towers with such uncensored terror that its date has become the most memorable of the twenty-first century. But the event that has made a more profound impact on human destiny than all the wars, the empires and the technological change put together, took place out of sight in a pre-dawn garden.

But that is the very reason why I insist that, despite its invisibility in present-day culture, the empty tomb must be recognized as a sign of the times. Jesus gave a warning to his own generation that his resurrection was the only sign they would need and the only sign they would get. Pharisees had come to him challenging him to perform yet another miracle as a sign of his divinity, but he refused angrily: 'You cannot interpret the signs of the times. A wicked and adulterous generation looks for a miraculous sign, but none will be given it except the sign of Jonah.'[7] Jonah was, of course, the prophet who in the ancient Jewish story had been swallowed by a fish and spent three days in its deathly inside before emerging from its mouth on to the shore of the Mediterranean Sea, alone but alive. Jesus was to be the new Jonah, emerging into life from the jaws of death. Silent and scarcely noticed!

Silent and scarcely noticed in our society is precisely what the empty tomb needs to be if it is to have any meaning. In our own lives the 'crucifixion' events are loud and public, degrading and fearful. They are as bitter as winter. We are bereaved with an awfulness that tears our spirits as cruelly as if our organs themselves were torn. Relationships break up with anguish and tears and ache. Redundancies come harshly, with recrimination and in full view of our colleagues. Violence breaks into our lives suddenly, unjustly and with great dread. Pain makes our very bones and muscles shout aloud at us.

But resurrection does not come like that. It comes silently and sometimes unseen. It comes unnoticed, like shoots stirring in the bulbs which tentatively push new life upward in the dark under the winter earth.

When I am bereaved, resurrection begins when I look at a photograph of the person whose loss has been so wounding, and the sight of it unexpectedly brings a smile of joyful memory rather than a reopening of the wound. That is how God silently empties the tomb.

When relationships break up, resurrection begins when I realize (unbeknown to anyone else) that for the first time recently I am enjoying something because I am me, not because I am half of a partnership. That is how God silently empties the tomb.

When redundancy comes, resurrection begins when I

discover that I have done something new or different which genuinely fills me with the measure of my own worth, rather than filling me with satisfaction at what my job is worth. That is how God silently empties the tomb.

The new life that follows violence might not even be noticed, because one day I revisit the scene and there is no fear. In fact, the memory of it does not occur to me. Sometimes resurrection is so quiet and private that it is an absence, not a presence.

And when pain is intolerable, resurrection begins when I slip away from the body that has limited and disabled me and, all by myself, step into the presence of God. That, of all ways, is how God silently brings new life out of a tomb.

Of course, this is not to deny the noisy celebration of the resurrection with which the church praises the risen Jesus on Easter morning. As Augustine, an African bishop in the fourth century, wrote: 'We are an Easter people, and Alleluia is our song.' But when our lives are not like that, when we feel the weight of life oppressively on our shoulders, it does not mean that the sign of the empty tomb has no meaning. It is those circumstances which most closely resemble the ground on which the resurrection first took place. And it may be that in those circumstances resurrection is already underway. Not with the stone being rolled away – that can come later amid great partying. But with life returning – inside the shroud, inside the cave, inside the darkness of the night.

This was the first reaction to the empty tomb to be written in the accounts that have survived for us to read in the Bible: 'Trembling and bewildered, the women went out and fled from the tomb. They said nothing to anyone, because they were afraid.'[8] Is that *really* a resurrection experience? Mixed emotions and confusion? Yes, actually! That was the resurrection experience of the first Sunday.

Later on the full victory of the empty tomb would be realized. Later on its triumph would sustain courageous faith while lions were roaring in the Coliseum; subservient faith when kings stepped up to the throne for their coronation; glorious faith when communion was consecrated in a grand cathedral; committed faith by a believer at his baptism; nervous faith by a student about to sit her exams; exploratory faith by a young man leaving home for the first time; thankful faith from someone who survived cancer; angry faith at the funeral of someone who didn't; desperate faith by a nation on whom bombs were dropping; anxious faith by a mother wondering why her daughter is not yet home from the nightclub at three in the morning; sustained faith by a couple enjoying their golden wedding anniversary; joyous faith by a band singing, 'He has risen, he has risen, Jesus is alive!'

That is how resurrection takes hold! But it is not how resurrection begins – this quietest of all revolutions.

One day the resurrection will be complete. We will take our place alongside Jesus in the presence of God. It will mean an eternity of justice restored, of peace made real, of healing made whole. That is when the signs of the present times will be revealed for what they really were. We will look back with gratitude on those which have pointed us toward values that are worthy and lasting. Those which turned out to be trivial distractions from the true purpose of being alive will long have slipped our memories. The sign of the empty tomb, whether it grows or diminishes in significance as the centuries roll past, will make us smile as we recognize how faintly it pointed us toward the fullness of what it actually means to be raised from the dead.

Leaving this decade's signs of the times behind, we will tread the path which Jesus alone has trod. I have no idea what it will be like. I don't think I want to know yet. It is altogether possible that when our turn comes to meet with God it will be with fanfares, triumph and spectacle. That would, of course, be wonderful! But it would suit me very well to be able to enter God's presence in an altogether different way. In the manner of Jesus' resurrection – without fuss, without noise, with a certain knowledge that the purposes of life are made plain once and for all, and whispering in astonishment: 'Glory, glory, glory, glory!'

Notes

1 http://emptytomb.hypermart.net
2 John 10:11.
3 Genesis 8:11.
4 Piero della Francesca, *The Resurrection*, Museo Civico, San Sepulcro, Italy.
5 C. S. Lewis, *The Discarded Image*, Cambridge University Press, 1964.
6 Alice Meynell, 'Easter Night', *Collected Poems*, Burns Oates and Washbourne, 1923.
7 Matthew 16:3.
8 Mark 16:8.